MW00653815

"Dr. Priya Nalkur makes the concepts of inclusive leadership accessible and easy to understand. This book based on truth-telling is a necessary read!"

DEEPA PURUSHOTHAMAN, author of *The First, the Few, the Only: How Women of Color Can Redefine Power in Corporate America*

"The principles of leadership and inclusivity in this book have revolutionized our company's culture. I was so impressed with Dr. Nalkur and her approach that I hired her to teach JEDI for Leaders© to our entire company nationally, across multiple field offices. Her safe yet challenging method of teaching these concepts had an amazing impact on the way our company communicates. Priya made a lasting change in our corporate culture."

JONATHAN CROSS, CEO of Cross Financial Corporation

"Becoming a more inclusive leader is a challenge that's both timely and evergreen. Priya does a remarkable job of highlighting the urgency for making powerful, positive change while also making the case for improvement despite our inevitable (and very human) missteps and mistakes along the way. This is a must-read for anyone in a current or future leadership role."

DEBORAH GRAYSON RIEGEL, author of *Go to Help: 31 Strategies to Offer, Ask For, and Accept Help*

"Priya Nalkur brings insight, wisdom, and a generosity of spirit to one of the most important challenges of our time. Engaging and beautifully written, this book takes us on a journey to become inclusive leaders—a crooked path that requires both failure and forgiveness. You won't be able to put it down!"

MARTHA FREYMANN MISER, Ph.D., founder and president, Aduro Consulting, LLC

"This book proves that Priya truly practices what she preaches: intelligence, common sense, and understanding of inclusiveness delivered in a warm, kind, inviting way. Reading the book made me feel like I was having a magical one-on-one coaching session with Priya, where every minute I feel like I learn something new that ultimately makes me feel better. I kept saying out loud, 'Yes,' 'That's right,' and 'So true!' while reading that my kids thought I was having a conversation with someone! I bet you'll do the same, so don't miss out."

LAKSHMI BALACHANDRA, Ph.D., Associate Professor of Entrepreneurship, Babson College

"Dr. Nalkur strikes the difficult balance of exposing us to our growth edge without triggering our defensiveness or shame response. As a result, readers can openly engage with the insights to maximize reflection and learning, instead of protecting our own fragility."

BEN OLDS, Managing Partner, HAVEN Human Assets

"Dr. Priya Nalkur's book is a leadership game-changer. As a beneficiary of her insightful coaching, skillfully penned in this book, she unveils the essence of inclusive leadership—embrace your values, lead with empathy, celebrate our differences, and watch the profound impact ripple through your surroundings. A must-read for those aspiring to lead with authenticity and inclusivity!"

ABBAS KAZIMI, Chief Business Officer, Nimbus Therapeutics

"Catalyze your ability to lead through inclusivity! Through this book, Priya shines a light on how to practically connect, empathize, learn, and build upon your own humanity, and to transform it into your source of power for positive change."

LUIS RODRIGUEZ, CEO, Raisa Energy

www.amplifypublishing.com

Stumbling Towards Inclusion: Finding Grace in Imperfect Leadership

Written in collaboration with Scott Doyle
www.scottwdoyle.net

For more information, please contact:
Amplify Publishing, an imprint of Amplify Publishing Group
620 Herndon Parkway, Suite 220
Herndon, VA 20170
info@amplifypublishing.com

Library of Congress Control Number: 2023920945
CPSIA Code: PRV1223A
ISBN-13: 978-1-63755-881-2

Printed in the United States

To A and Z, nestled between you is a universe of letters, stories, songs, and dreams. You are the voice.

STUMBLING TOWARDS INCLUSION

FINDING GRACE IN IMPERFECT LEADERSHIP

PRIYA NALKUR, ED.D.

amplify

an imprint of Amplify Publishing Group

CONTENTS

PREFACE

I want to inspire those who inspire me most, seventeen-year-old me wrote earnestly in my journal. I had been thinking a lot about my future and wanted to do something meaningful. Growing up and going to school as a brown girl in a Canadian town that wasn't terribly diverse made me want to break out of what felt like a very confined life. I wanted to be accepted, seen, and understood. In my awkward way, I had touched on something that wouldn't become clear to me until much later: there is a reciprocity to inspiration and influence, and it is a two-way street.

This truth came home to me in a powerful way more than two decades later. I had started my own coaching firm with a mission to help business people become more inclusive leaders. I was coaching a man who was CEO of a large national business. Michael had inherited a good deal of privilege and influence and had stepped into the role with apparent ease.

And then George Floyd was murdered. Michael was one of those CEOs who instantly knew that this was a historic inflection point. This was a moment for business leaders to step up and address issues of racism, bias, exclusion, and inequity head-on. The reckoning that was widely spoken of at the time couldn't just happen in the streets; it had to happen in the boardroom as well.

Suddenly Michael wasn't so sure of himself. He didn't know if he was ready, if he was up to the moment. "Why do I have to be the leader at this time?" he asked me. But he did it anyway. Embracing the mission of inclusive leadership without reservation, he led with vulnerability and a willingness to make mistakes. He invited dialogue, he invited conflict, and he invited situations in which he was sure to stumble, yet in which he was also sure to learn and grow. Even though he might get burned, he stepped into the fire, knowing it would make him a better leader.

It did. He emerged with a new and hard-won confidence that ran deep, a certain fearlessness. He now has a presence I see vividly in the most inclusive leaders. That presence is borne of the process and journey—you don't get there without allowing others to influence, shape, inspire, and teach you. Allowing yourself to be influenced by others—especially those with backgrounds and experiences very different from your own—becomes a profound form of influence in its own right. The reciprocity is contagious.

You don't have to be a CEO to wield this influence. You don't need formal power. All you need is a voice. And a willingness to step into that fire and be changed by it.

I passionately believe in the mission of inclusion. The world provides evidence every day of how badly this work is needed, how that basic human need to be accepted, welcomed, and understood so often goes unmet. I wanted to write a book that clearly established the urgency of this mission and that captured the fire in my belly around this cause. But I also wanted to write a forgiving book. In my travels around companies and organizations in North America and across the world, I've come across so many leaders who *do* understand what is at stake. And that is precisely what keeps them from speaking up and stepping into the fray. They worry they are not up to the challenge. They worry they are not ready, or too late. They are scared that they will say the wrong thing.

So I wanted to write a book that normalizes mistakes. I wanted to lay out a path in which human fallibility isn't just an unfortunate part of the journey but intrinsic to it.

I wanted to write a book that was equal parts fire and forgiveness.

———

THIS BOOK BEGINS WITH A HEAVY FOCUS on my own story—much more so than I am normally comfortable with. In fact, devoting so much space to very personal stories made me decidedly uncomfortable, and I thought twice about whether that was the best way to open the book. I am uncomfortable sharing who I am with you—with anyone really. But I persisted through that discomfort for several reasons.

First, I have often found that growth and new insight live in the places where we are willing to get a bit uncomfortable. Most of the time, the discomfort signals to me that I'm on the edge of something new—an awakening, a crossover, an idea. Discomfort can be a useful friction. The upside is not always immediate; sometimes those new ideas spark with a slow burn. But the discomfort eventually yields something, and to me, that's important.

Second, the ideas in this book have come from who I am and where I've been. The context matters and will help to make sense of my perspective and why I think certain things are worth exploring. Respect for identity is at the heart of inclusive leadership, and identity comes from lived experience. So does voice, one of the most important tools for an inclusive leader.

Finally, I am keenly aware that *my* story—as a woman of color, a dual national with a complicated immigration history, a divorcée, and a mother—has been historically excluded, underrepresented, and underestimated. Fully coming into my identity was a long process. Like all so-called minorities, I felt the pressure to assimilate to the norm and to the dominant culture—at the expense of exploring my Indian heritage and discovering who I was. I am encouraged to be one of a small but growing number of women of color writing and speaking out about inclusion. But to be sure, ours is not the dominant narrative; I feel a responsibility to share my story and do my part to diversify the conversation.

I hope that sharing my own story—as uncomfortable as it initially was—frees you up to do the same with yours. One of my maxims is: Great leaders know their own stories. Really well. And they are willing to courageously share them. Writing this book forced me to live out that advice and get comfortable in a new way with my own story. In fact, I learned to really like that story. These experiences turned me into the coach I am. And made me realize that my calling in life is to bring greater inclusion and belonging into the workplace.

Later in this book, I will share the principles and practices of inclusive leadership I have distilled over the years. I close the book with stories of my clients' triumphs and struggles in their journeys to become more inclusive leaders. I suspect you will see yourself in some of those stories. I hope that provides some guidance and perspective for you on your own journey.

Let's begin.

INTRODUCTION

In writing on a topic as potentially vast and far-reaching as diversity and inclusion, I had to be very clear about the book I was writing. I had to decide what I could and could not do within these pages, which can only cover so much.

So, first: this is not a handbook for defeating bias and inherited privilege in society and the world at large. That larger cause is one I believe in, which is one reason that justice comes first in the JEDI© acronym.* I believe that diversity, equity, and inclusion (DEI) initiatives in the workplace should be cognizant of and informed by larger struggles in society. The very language with which we think about these issues continues to be shaped by those struggles, and historically excluded people bring their experiences of those struggles into the workplace. But the purpose of this book is to take on the essential but more narrowly defined task of helping leaders, like yourself, be more inclusive and build more inclusive cultures within their businesses, organizations, and communities.

---

* The JEDI© (justice, equity, diversity, and inclusion) training package is something I developed for my company, RoundTable. This will be discussed more later.

Second, this book will not include an exhaustive breakdown of the various kinds of difference; of the systems of privilege, bias, and exclusion that accompany those differences; or of the nuances in the challenge of creating inclusion and belonging for those affected communities. However, understanding the geography of difference and diversity *is* important. One of the ongoing projects of being an inclusive leader is diversifying your reading, and your cultural diet generally. You need to take in the experiences and perspectives of people whose lives are very different from your own. Assessing the diversity of your reading, your media consumption, and your personal and professional networks is a useful exercise for someone aspiring to inclusive leadership.[*]

The kinds of differences you will encounter in your own workplace and community will vary greatly. The constant will be the kind of culture that can meet, see, and embrace those differences. This is why I stress developing a relativistic mindset, learning to see through a culturally sensitive lens, and practicing cultural humility. Those leadership skills will go a long way toward helping you create a culture of inclusion. As you grow to become more inclusive and diverse as a leader, you will invariably deepen your understanding of specific kinds of differences.

"NATURE LOVES SMALL ERRORS."[†] Nassim Nicholas Taleb's words snagged my mind as I was writing this book. I instinctively sensed they were somehow relevant. I kept circling back to that short phrase, and I realized

---

[*] In RoundTable's JEDI for Leaders© training, we call this a "self-audit."
[†] Nassim Nicholas Taleb, *Antifragile: Things That Gain from Disorder* (New York: Random House Publishing Group, 2014).

that a couple of my core convictions intersect with those four simple words.

The first is the lens of developmental psychology that is now so central to how I view the world—specifically the challenge of inclusive leadership. It is a philosophy that embraces our fallibility as intrinsic to learning and growing. We don't evolve *in spite* of our errors but *because* of them. We should come to love them, not shun them.

The evolution I am talking about is emotional, social, and intellectual. Taleb, of course, is referring to another kind of evolution, the long and slow process by which all organisms on Earth, including humans, developed over time into their current form. Biological evolution is all about trial and error. Genetic mutations and modifications come about randomly and by accident and then are given a real-life trial in the field of survival. Traits that help a species thrive are passed on and persist.

Which brings me to my second conviction that Taleb's words embody: trial and error—the heart of the scientific method. I have always loved the spirit of inquiry and curiosity that characterizes scientific research. Errors are treated not as mistakes to be regretted but as valuable sources of information. The scientist views errors as data. Unlike in natural selection, errors are not random in the scientific method. You go in with a hunch, a theory, and you test it. As the data comes back to you, you calibrate your method and approach, and the errors get smaller and less frequent. You love small errors because they tell you you're on the right track.

As you will see, I often invoke the scientific method as an instructive model for how to approach the challenge of inclusive leadership. In order to become places where a diverse range of employees can all thrive and belong, organizations must undergo their own evolution. There is no escaping the necessity of trial and error in this process of adaptive change. As it turns out, the scientific method depends on well-developed intuition. Science and intuition dance together to make smaller errors. And just like the scientist, you as a business leader can adapt and calibrate to keep your errors small and manageable. You, too, can learn to love them and the lessons they teach.

I initially doubted that the larger context of Taleb's phrase was relevant to this book. But here, too, the more I dug into it, the more it resonated. In his book, Taleb argues that we should aspire to be more than simply resilient, to bounce back from difficulty and disruption. Nature is his model. Apply stress to an organism or an ecosystem, and often it comes back stronger. Rather than fear uncertainty and volatility, he says, we should embrace it and allow it to instruct us.

———

NOW YOU MIGHT BE WONDERING what this has to do with inclusive leadership. A running theme of this book is that by taking on the challenge of being a more inclusive leader, you will end up becoming a better leader period. All of the skill sets essential for leadership in today's environment—emotional intelligence, relationship-building, cultivating psychological safety—are precisely those that the work of inclusion will require of you and bring out in you.

Since 1987, it has been a given (bordering on cliché) that leaders must learn to manage a VUCA world—a world characterized by volatility, uncertainty, complexity, and ambiguity. No challenge you will face as a leader will better prepare you to handle volatility than the work of inclusion. Our sense of identity—and our feelings as to whether that identity is fully seen, heard, and respected, or not—represent some of the most powerful and raw aspects of being a human. How these dynamics play out in organizations and in society as a whole is fraught with volatility and potential land mines.

If the events of the early 2020s are any guide to the future, the many issues wrapped up in the goal of greater diversity, equity, inclusion, and belonging will continue to be major stressors on employers and organizational leaders. The murder of George Floyd in the United States was a game changer, igniting political protests across the world and also rocking the workplace. Some leaders met the challenge; many stumbled.

The Great Resignation, the largest mass exit from the workforce in decades, sprang from numerous factors. But surveys revealed that employees leaving their jobs often cited the lack of belonging and inclusion as a significant reason. An inclusive culture is no longer a nice extra, a thin line between a relatively content employee and a truly satisfied one. Increasingly, it will determine whether you retain top talent or even attract them in the first place.

The best leaders will take on the challenge of building an inclusive workplace—with all of the inevitable messiness and ambiguity of that effort—with fearless gusto, not reluctantly or defensively. They will allow the raw emotion and volatility of the issues involved to instruct them and forge them into better leaders, their companies into better companies. They will lead boldly but also with vulnerability; they will learn to love their small errors and to grant themselves and others the grace to stumble along the way.* They will emerge from that struggle better able to

---

* We hope to keep our errors small and the damage limited, but unfortunately, that is not always the case. Sometimes our mistakes will cause real harm. Sometimes that harm will be difficult or impossible to repair. And apologizing, while helpful if done the right way, does not undo the harm. All of which is to say: we need to be mindful and intentional about our words and actions—while at the same time not letting this awareness make us overly cautious. A tough balancing act, I know! But this book will give you the tools to prevent, minimize, and reduce harm, and give you the room to make and learn from mistakes.

create a great organizational culture and to meet whatever unseen challenges arise in the future.

Great inclusive leaders are great leaders, period.

PART I

FINDING (AND OWNING) MY VOICE

1

THREE STORIES OF BELONGING

My introduction (at least the first that I distinctly remember) to the power of belonging, and not belonging, was a rude one.

It was 1982, and I was the only brown kid in my Ottawa kindergarten class. I was not unaware of that fact, but neither would I say I was hyper aware of it. It was a fact of life, but it didn't define my identity, or my standing with my classmates.

All that changed one fall day as we prepared to pose as a group for our school photo. Kindergarten tends to be highly regimented, and we were lined up—as we were frequently instructed to do—from shortest to tallest. Which meant that I was standing in line next to a boy named Sebastian.

As we were getting ready to march into the gym to pose for our class portrait, he turned to me and said, "You can't be in the picture. You're brown. You'll ruin it."

Looking down at my arm and seeing my brown skin, I realized he must be right. Matter-of-factly, I stayed to the side of the gym while the rest of the class strode to take their places. Our teacher, Mrs. Haley, noticed I had been left behind and came over to me to ask what was wrong. I told her what Sebastian had said.

Mrs. Haley didn't reprimand Sebastian. She didn't make a big deal of it at all. She simply invited me to rejoin the group and to sit on her lap while we posed for the school photo. As the photographer was preparing to snap the shot, she turned to Sebastian and said, "Isn't it great that we get to sit together as a class?"

I should point out, as a side note, that getting to sit on her lap was a big deal. It was a place of pride. Even at a young four years of age, I was already reading when I started kindergarten, so I was ahead of the rest of the class. Numerous times, Mrs. Haley had me come to the front of the class, sit on her lap, and read aloud to the class.

There are a number of notable things about this story. I notice, even as I am writing this, that I have chosen to open a section about finding my voice with an incident in which I did not speak up, but where someone spoke up for me. Sometimes we find our voice when someone else models using theirs.

Looking back on this day, the coach in me is highly cognizant of what Mrs. Haley did and did not do to defuse a potentially divisive and uncomfortable moment. I recognize what she did and did not say.

Another notable thing is that this is as much my mother's recounting of the episode as my own. I don't have a vivid sense of that day. It didn't wound or traumatize me. I very much took it in stride. My response to initially being left out of the class photo was, *Oh, so this is how it's going to be.*

My mother, however, knew it was a big deal. She retells the story often and with great pride. She marks this as the moment when my activism began. She doesn't frame my matter-of-fact acceptance of being left out as weakness or passivity but as a kind of strength, a stoic refusal to let prejudice and bias get the best of me. At some point, I'm not sure where my mother's memory of the incident ends and mine begins.

This was not my last run-in with Sebastian. He continued to target me over the next two years as we all moved on to first then second grade. I remember one time during recess when he got in my face as I was eating an Indian sweet my mother had prepared for me, pistachio burfi. He got real close and said, "Ewww . . . That's disgusting. Indians eat soap!" He spat on the food, but I continued to eat it anyway. Burfi, a kind of sweet pistachio fudge, is a rich, mouth-pleasing indulgence that is a celebratory food in Indian culture. It is topped with a thin layer of silver as if to underscore how special it is. I was not about to toss it or waste a single bite.

But here's the kicker: I remember Sebastian as brown. He was not, as I was, identifiably ethnic in a way that clearly marked him as "other." But he was darker than the other kids. He was short, which is why he was standing in line next to me in kindergarten. And he had trouble writing out his own name, which is longer and more complicated than other first names.

As an adult with more perspective on the situation, I realize these aspects of Sebastian's life probably made him feel as though he didn't belong. And, in classic bully-fashion, he dealt with his hurt feelings by trying to hurt mine. The feeling of not belonging is a powerful one and can perpetuate the cycle of exclusion.

———

The incident in kindergarten was a fairly cut-and-dry example of belonging and not belonging, of inclusion and exclusion. Flash forward a few years later to an episode in my life where the picture gets a little more complicated.

My sister Sonal (just shy of two years older than me) and I were both enrolled at the age of six or seven in Indian classical dance classes. The classes themselves, and our occasional performances, were significant gatherings for the local Indian community. Our instructor, Sheela, was a family friend. Everyone knew everyone else. (In the years since, some non-Indians have started taking the classes. But at that point, it was purely an extension and expression of the local South Indian community.)

The form of dance we were studying, Bharatanatyam, is the oldest classical dance tradition in India. It is mentioned in several ancient texts, and expresses a number of South Indian religious, cultural, and spiritual themes, drawing on Hinduism among other traditions. The British colonial government banned Bharatanatyam in 1910.

Bharatanatyam is a demanding dance form. It involves a series of swift and precise movements. The upper torso is fixed while the legs bend into squats and other difficult positions accompanied by intricate and percussive footwork. While the rest of the body is engaged in all of this highly athletic activity, the eyes, face, and hands are communicating the emotional heart of the story, often drawn from Hindu myths. We got in quite the workout, and by the end of class we were soaked in sweat.

On the face of it, this was an opportunity for my sister and me, along with our parents, to escape our customary minority status and enjoy being a majority among our own people.* Also, my parents were trying to strike a delicate balance between adopting Western values and culture while remaining close to our Indian traditions. But in a way that sometimes eludes attention, identity is not a single thing. It is layered, and it is multiple, existing along several different planes at the same time.

Along one plane, we were all part of the local South Indian community and as such were united by our shared heritage. But in other ways, my family and I were members of a distinct minority—a minority within a minority, even.

My family hails from the community of Konkani speakers in India. Konkani is one of twenty-two languages officially recognized in the Indian

---

* As we will discuss later, *minority* is a problematic term.

constitution. Konkani speakers are a fairly small community themselves, but there are numerous subdivisions even within this community. Prominent among Konkani speakers are three Hindu Brahmin subcastes, all under the umbrella of *Saraswat Brahmins.* My family is from the *Chitrapur Saraswats,* who are by far the smallest of the three. Globally, our community now stands at about twenty-five thousand. At an annual North American Konkani convention, we are a clear minority.

So, yes—my family is a minority (Chitrapur) within a minority (Konkani) within a minority (South Indian). All of that played out for my sister and me in our classical Indian dance classes through the medium of language, one of the most potent and identifiable indicators of culture and identity. We loved Sheela, our instructor. But she was a strict taskmaster. Bharatanatyam is a rigorous and demanding dance form, and she would frequently scold the students. Yet she did so in two languages: Kannada for the rest of the class, English for Sonal and me. It clearly and viscerally marked us as different. In fact, Sheela would joke that English did not allow her to scold us in the precise and cutting manner in which she scolded the other students.

None of which detracts from what a tremendous and positive experience these dance classes were for Sonal and me, for our family, for the entire community. But yes—identity (and therefore belonging) is complicated and layered and multiple. We will see this fact play out through this book.

The story of our classical Indian dance classes segues nicely into the final of this opening trio of stories about the nuances of identity and belonging. Sonal was better at the theatrical and artistic elements of Bharatanatyam, but I responded strongly to the athleticism of it all. It was in athletics that

I was first told I was really good at something.

Now, what does all of this have to do with identity and belonging?

My sister and I, you see, belonged to another club: that of the "model minority." The model minority trope—a combination of myth and stereotype that may seem positive and complimentary on its face but is in fact destructive, divisive, and deeply problematic—is largely associated with Asians. As such, immigrants of Indian descent (India being part of Southwest Asia) are caught up in this.

At the core of the myth is the expectation that we would excel academically and then professionally, and that financial success would be part of the latter. We would succeed in not just any profession, we would be doctors—medical doctors, specifically—lawyers, or engineers. We would follow what I have come to call the model minority playbook.

As my sister and I grew up, that meant our education took priority over everything else. Schooling came at the expense of all the other activities that "normal" (i.e., white) kids engaged in, such as summer camp, visiting grandparents, and cottage road trips. So, I was already "other" by virtue of having brown skin and clearly being from an ethnic minority. Layered on top of this, my behavior and social life, which was largely limited to the Indian community in Ottawa, also marked me as other and not quite normal.

Strangely enough, it was athletics that led me down a path whereby I was able to depart from—if not fully escape—that playbook.

I responded well to the physical demands of classical Indian dance. And then I discovered swimming. I so vividly remember the words of my first competitive swim coach, Paul Jensen. He said, "She has so much potential."

So much potential. These words were gold to a young girl of whom so much was expected. I was doing fine at school, but aside from being an early reader with very good language skills, it wasn't like I was excelling.

At swimming, I did indeed excel. Swimming also helped me internalize habits of discipline and focus that, for a while, deserted me in school. I was doing good enough in school—until suddenly I wasn't. In eleventh grade, my grades fell off a cliff. I was failing everything except English. No one could explain it.

My parents took me out of school and sent me to India to complete my final year of high school by correspondence. There, largely out of desperation, I finally learned how to study properly. It wasn't so much the change of environment (although perhaps that helped some) but the prospect of failing out of high school and not getting into college that was a wake-up call.

I responded and got into university. Just barely. And not at an Ivy League school like my sister but at the University of Western Ontario. There, my interest in athletics led me to pursue a degree in kinesiology, a kind of advanced form of physical education.

I had departed pretty significantly from the model minority playbook, but my parents cut me some slack because, it turns out, my sister was running into her own difficulties. In high school, Sonal had excelled in the liberal arts, which is where her real passion lay. But she was also excellent at math. In response to our parents' expectations and the larger expectations of our South Indian heritage, she enrolled in the engineering program at Cornell. It did not work out. Her heart simply wasn't in it, and two years into the program, she left.

Although my parents still had high expectations for both of us, they worried that perhaps they had been too hard on us. They reluctantly accepted my decision to study kinesiology*. They supported Sonal as she

---

* At the orientation for new students and families at Western, I remember my dad asking the academic advisor, "What exactly *is* kinesiology anyway?"

changed course to study English at McMaster University.

We had earned a degree of wiggle room in the path anticipated for us. Yet neither of us fully escaped the playbook. We were both pursuing (in my parents' view) nonstandard careers—but it was still expected that we would excel. The fact that I later pursued postgraduate studies at Yale and Harvard helped compensate for the fact that I got a doctorate in psychology and not medicine.

Still, the pull of the model minority myth and ethos dies hard. Sonal has a doctorate in sociology and multiple masters degrees. She is accomplished, respected, and thriving. All the same, even now my mother will inquire of her, "Do you ever think about going back and finishing that engineering degree?"

Belonging to certain identities and communities can lift us up and define us in empowering ways. It can also limit and constrain us. Learning to belong fully to ourselves (and within that, to find our voice) involves a delicate dance of moving in and out of various identities as we chart our own course through life.

Identity and belonging are multiple. They are fluid and evolving.

2

TWO TABLES, MANY TEACHERS

I grew up on the west side of Ottawa in a neighborhood called Crystal Beach, which is on the southern shore of the Ottawa River—Quebec is to the north on the other side. In my neighborhood, two dead-end streets, ours and the adjacent one, formed a kind of vast outdoor playground for us. Because there was no through traffic, it was safe for my sister and me and all of the other neighborhood kids to play outside. And in the summertime especially, we did, from morning until dusk.

It was a safe neighborhood, where we could walk to the bus stop by ourselves or to school or to the park. There was a corner store called Beckers where we went whenever we had a little pocket money to buy a pack of gum or an ice cream cone.

We would go in and out of one another's homes as if they were our own. While it took my parents a while to find their way in this new community, over the years, our home became a gathering spot: for family, for my parents' friends, for our friends. Within the neighborhood, our floor-model television set established itself as the communal viewing site for major world events: in other words, the release of a new Cyndi Lauper video or the rescue of Baby Jessica.*

More substantive gatherings often took place over meals lovingly prepared by my mother and around one of two tables that became focal points for our shared life while Sonal and I were growing up, which have since become central to family lore.

So much of our family life—so many cherished memories—happened around our big kitchen table. We had regular dinners there, did homework, cut cookies, wrapped presents, did arts and crafts, and had hard family conversations. There was nothing fancy or special about it. It had metal legs and a shiny fake wood top. It wasn't at all sturdy, but it somehow held the weight of all the activity and gathering that happened around it.

In the dining room, we had a larger oak table. Although it was sturdier than the kitchen table, it, too, was flawed, with one side that sloped noticeably. I remember how, in contrast to the constant clutter of the kitchen table, my parents made sure the dining room table looked nice when it wasn't being used, decorated perhaps with a vase of fresh flowers. And when we had gatherings that exceeded the capacity of the table (we could comfortably sit only six), I remember the effort and resourcefulness that went into fitting everyone in. We'd pull up the piano bench with a phone book for me to sit on. Or a stool or even lawn chairs still covered in grass clippings. We always made room for everyone. Everyone had a seat at the table.

Our first Christmas in Ottawa was a solitary one. My parents were still trying to figure out the holiday and how it was observed in Canada. But they made up for it, and then some, in subsequent years. The following year, they hosted Christmas for all of their local Indian friends. Large

------

* An eighteen-month-old girl who fell into her aunt's well in 1987. Her dramatic rescue took over two days and captivated the world. The incident happened in Texas, where I would later end up myself.

dinner gatherings became somewhat of a regular occasion at our house. My mother loved hosting, and these dinners energized her and brought out a playful even theatrical side of her.

She took great pride in her cooking and always cooked too much—we would have leftovers for days, which gave my sister and me an excuse to have our friends over. She started planning the menu a couple of weeks in advance, so we knew some of what she was cooking. But then she always had a surprise for us: a special dish that would only be revealed at mealtime, eliciting cries of, "You made *ras malai!*" which delighted her to no end. During the meals, she was effusive and loud and a gifted storyteller.

My father was less effusive and more of a quiet connector, but he, too, loved these gatherings and liked to perform (he came from a family of performers). He would make a special effort to connect people over a common interest. He has performed magic tricks for as long as I can remember, and he loved breaking those out during our New Year's Eve party. He would also lead us—adults and kids alike—in word games like charades. And it all happened around the dining room table.

Both tables stayed with us for my entire childhood, even when they were damaged and it seemed it might be best to replace them. Just recently, my mother asked me if I wanted to ship the kitchen table to my home in Austin.

My parents were my first teachers, my first coaches. My mother taught me to read at a very early age (which is how I ended up on Mrs. Haley's lap reading to my kindergarten class). My father drilled Sonal and me in math.

I had several other coaches and teachers whose influence in my life I simply can't overstate. You've met one of them, Sheela, who taught Sonal and me classical Indian dance.

Then there was Paul Jensen, my competitive swimming coach. Before I dive into everything he did for me, I should point out that my swim activities were entirely unconnected to school. So I did not enjoy any special status as an athlete among my classmates. In fact, for a while it was quite the opposite. In junior high, being regarded as "cool" meant being good at athletics. However, being good at athletics meant getting the seal of approval from Mr. Spence, the school gym teacher. And in his eyes, I most decidedly did not measure up.

There was no objective reason for this. In gym class, I performed as well as or better than other students but consistently was awarded a C. Once, I bested the previous school record in the long jump. Mr. Spence insisted there had been a measurement error and asked that I do it again. The only explanation for my poor grades in gym class—despite being athletically accomplished—is that I was the one brown girl in class. Continuing into high school, I did well at track and at cross-country—in fact, I am in the school hall of fame. But I was never celebrated as an athlete at school.

Swimming was different. From the start, Paul Jensen believed in me, pushed me, got the most out of me. I started at the age of eight and almost immediately excelled. My best events were the one- and two-hundred-meter backstroke and the one-hundred-meter breaststroke. Later I added the one-hundred-meter freestyle to my repertoire. I accumulated many medals and trophies over the years. But with the exception of one girl who I very much wanted to beat (and rarely did), it wasn't about interpersonal competition. I was competing with myself. Hitting a personal best is what really fueled me. When I did so, I was not demonstrative. I would beam quietly.

Paul was an unlikely coach in some respects. He was short and didn't swim himself. But he had an innate passion for coaching young people. He was strict. He pushed us as individuals, and he and I certainly enjoyed a special connection. But he stressed *team* above all else, especially at competitions. He insisted we sit as a bloc in the stands, wearing club colors, waving banners, and cheering our teammates on at the top of our lungs. Paul would stand at the edge of the pool, his face red from exhorting us on.

I swam as a member of various community clubs. I found Paul at the Ottawa-Carleton Kingfish Swim Club at the Nepean Sportsplex. When he moved on to the Boys & Girls Club, so did I. We spent a year in Saudi Arabia (my father had a job working for Saudi Telecom) where I swam in the Canadian Swim Club and continued to excel. When we returned to Ottawa, I initially lost track of Paul. (There was no Internet on which to look him up!) Yet one day, when I was standing at the bus stop, Paul just happened to drive by in his car. "Priya, you're back from Saudi!" We reconnected, and I began swimming with him at Bayshore Barracudas Swim Club.

The finances of this club were public, and my parents were astonished to find that Paul paid himself only $12,000 a year. So one day, my parents had Paul over for dinner and politely asked how he stayed financially afloat. It turned out he had a side gig working at a store called Sports Experts. He did it so he could afford to coach, which was his passion. He had no degree and few other options for making ends meet.

I don't want to characterize the life Paul had fashioned for himself as some kind of dead end. He was a model of commitment and following a passion at all costs—honestly, a worthy pursuit. Looking back, I think Paul could have been successful in conventional terms; he was a gifted coach with unparalleled dedication to his craft. But without the "right" education and social capital, his future was limited.

Though Paul didn't have a *financially* successful coaching career, I believe he was a wonderfully successful *coach*. Paul embodied many qualities of a great leader: he was passionate, dedicated, and committed first to the people he led rather than to his own gain. No amount of schooling can teach these qualities. I'm endlessly grateful for the example Paul set, and I aspire to these traits in my own coaching.

As do many parents, ours got Sonal and me to study piano at a young age. It didn't stick, not at first anyway. In elementary school, we had a teacher who came over once a week and said, "Good job!" no matter how terribly we played. I had no motivation to practice or excel.

When we started high school, my father decided to give it another shot. He called the Royal Conservatory of Music and asked them to recommend a teacher. Mrs. Pansy Lin was the unequivocal response. "She's the best," they said. She already had too many students and had turned down her fair share. My father persisted and begged her to take on my sister and me. Finally she relented. Her fees were steep, but my dad wanted the best for us.

She turned out to be phenomenal, worth every penny. Along with Paul Jensen, she was probably my best childhood teacher. To her I credit a deep love and appreciation for music, along with a great ear that I have to this day. She was tough, and I was a little afraid of her. But she really made a musician out of me (and Sonal as well). I practiced an hour a day when I was studying with her. Our classes took place at her house, in a tiny room that nonetheless held two pianos. On rare occasions, which I looked forward to and cherished, she would accompany me on her piano. She played beautifully. Beyond her wonderful music instruction, she took an interest in our academics and in our Indian dance. It turns out she herself had been a star athlete when she was young.

Mrs. Lin was small, round, and old, and spoke in a thick Chinese accent. She was sweet and funny and strict. Unlike Paul who was intense and in-your-face, her teaching approach was subtle and indirect, favoring stories, metaphors, and demonstration. She would begin lessons beside me at the piano with long, elaborate—and often funny—stories designed to impress on me the importance of hard work, practice, and appreciating music. Nothing could substitute effort, she said, and she had an uncanny ability to divine if I had skipped a day of practice. I can still hear her kindly admonishing me, "I think you missed a practice this week." She never lost patience with us, but it was always clear that it was her way or no way. When it came to my piano playing, I did not have a back-and-forth with her; I listened and played.

3

ROLE-PLAYING

These coaches and teachers made such an impression on me—indeed, the whole enterprise and mission of coaching and teaching seems to have struck a chord from the start—that I began, at a very young age, pretending to be a teacher and coach. As I prepared to work on this book, I asked my sister and parents if, looking back, they could identify any "seeds" of the coach I would become as an adult tucked away in my childhood. It didn't exactly take a lot of digging. Without naming or being conscious of what I was doing at the time, it's clear now that I was experimenting with taking on the role of teacher or coach at every opportunity.

Looking back at these instances, it's almost hard to know where to start. My past fairly screams out, "I am meant to be a coach!" But start somewhere we must, so let's begin with my passion for reliving and reenacting tests and homework. Early on, when I was doing well in school (before I inexplicably wasn't), I developed this habit, almost a compulsion, of coming home and rewriting the tests and assignments I had completed that day at school. (Nerd alert!)

There were a couple of things going on here. First, I think I was simply reliving and savoring an experience I had found pleasing. I enjoyed being tested and welcomed the feedback that came with being graded. But I was also role-playing by adopting the role of the teacher. I reviewed work I had already completed, but now through the lens of a teacher, evaluating and figuring out how to instruct and motivate this young girl (me). When you think about it, it's not so weird. (Okay, it is a little weird.) We role-play all the time as kids: inventing scenarios and then adopting multiple roles, switching between them, trying on personas as if we were trying on clothes. We're trying to figure out what fits. And coaching and teaching fit me, to a tee.

My favorite workout with Paul Jensen was the Saturday morning swim, which ran from six to eight. For ninety minutes, he ran drills, and I loved those. But for the final thirty minutes, we played games that Paul had ingeniously contrived to push us and test us in the water, all while feeling we were playing. Sometimes we did relay races, sometimes obstacle courses or a game of water polo. He'd have us practice our starts and flip turns against the wall. These drills were fun but strenuous, especially after a full ninety-minute practice.

On occasion Paul would yell, without warning, "Meet me at the courts!" We'd have to jump out of the pool and meet him, still dripping with water, on the adjoining basketball court for a quick game of pickup. He loved basketball and emphasized the team aspect of it. Even though swimming was technically an individual sport, he saw it as a team sport and encouraged us to swim for each other, not for ourselves. For him, those Saturday morning sessions were very much about building community and team spirit.

When I got home from Saturday swim, I would shower, have some breakfast, and maybe watch cartoons for a while. Then I would head outside to that vast outdoor playground formed by our two dead-end streets where, when the weather allowed, we would run and play as long as there was light.

For the younger children, I would re-create the games Paul had led us through that morning in the pool. I would design intricate obstacle courses, using sprinklers, brooms, ladders—anything at hand in our dusty garages. I would instruct the younger kids, coach them, rate them, and urge them on just as my prized teachers and coaches did. It wasn't about power or judging them. It was about uplifting them, as others had lifted me up. It was my life's work, long before I realized it.

My sister, Sonal, reminds me how—however much I admired her, and I did at times follow her around like a little puppy—I didn't try to break in or prove myself with the older kids she hung out with. It seemed there were very few kids my age back then. They were either Sonal's age or older, or they were younger than me. And I chose to coach and mentor those I felt I had something to teach, and who were willing to follow me.

Even in my private playtime with Sonal, the same theme manifested itself. She wanted to play house. I said, "No, let's play school."

With me, of course, as the teacher.

4

SHY AND TIMID

Yes, I had my teachers and my coaches. I had my swimming and my nerdy routine of rewriting my schoolwork. I had my sister and my parents. But I struggled with loneliness and shyness. And unfortunately, Sebastian was not the last classmate to bully me.

I have distanced myself from a lot of those memories, just as I have with that day in the kindergarten gymnasium that I do not clearly recall. But my mother remembers these episodes well. There was a series of bullies—perhaps so many that I have suppressed my memory of them and distilled them in my mind to that one bully I do remember. Yet even with Sebastian, there are details my mother has had to remind me of. He didn't just say I was brown and didn't belong in the class photo. He said I was dirty and ugly.

I'm sure these words must have wounded me at the time. I was inclined to be quiet and introverted anyway, very much a contrast to my loud and outgoing older sister. But the bullying drove me deeper within myself. The process of learning to emerge from that place of refuge took years.

My shyness notwithstanding, one thing that did bring me pleasure and satisfaction (ever since those days of reading to the class while perched on Mrs. Haley's lap) was giving oral presentations. It was simply something I felt comfortable doing and knew I was good at. And years of piano recitals and Bharatanatyam performances helped me feel at home on stage. But this, too, is the source of another sour memory from these years.

Each year, we had a school speech contest that was a pretty big deal. You had to go through multiple rounds as some students advanced and others were eliminated. The winner of the school contest would later go on to participate in regional and national contests. I had participated in two previous contests and, despite doing well, hadn't won, even though many felt I should have. My mother knew how much the competition meant to me, and in fourth grade, she helped me a great deal with my speech. When I finished my speech, the feedback was clear and immediate: everyone present thought that I was the obvious winner. Yet I didn't even advance to the next round—I was passed over for a girl who had struggled to even complete her speech. When my parents picked me up later that day, I was in tears.

But this girl had an inside connection of sorts—and in that was an early lesson (though, of course, I didn't fully understand it until much later) in certain dynamics of inclusion and exclusion, and of the immigrant mindset. Her mother was a substitute teacher who worked frequently at the school. In the academic jargon I would later become conversant with, she had social capital and was not afraid to use it. My parents, by contrast, who were not on their native soil, never felt comfortable playing that inside game nor did they think it was theirs to play.

Before we can find or fully grow into our voice, I would later realize, we must claim the ground we stand on. More than once, I saw my parents hesitate to claim that ground and assert themselves. For example, when my sister was struggling at Cornell, I don't think it occurred to my parents to take the initiative to approach guidance counselors and academic advisers to find a solution short of dropping out (even as we watched our white friends' parents do that kind of thing all the time). For a long time, I internalized that reticence and the respect for authority that comes with it. I was afraid to rock the boat . . . until I wasn't.

———

Midway through my fourth-grade year, we left to live in Saudi Arabia, where my father's work took him. We returned a year later in the middle of fifth grade, and trying to reintegrate into the school community posed an additional challenge for a young girl who, for a host of reasons, was awkward, shy, and timid.

Further complicating matters, when we got back, it was decided that I could skip the rest of fifth grade, which meant I also had to adjust to an entirely new class. Academically I was able to keep up, but socially it set me apart even more than I already was.

Then another layer of isolation was thrown into the mix. I sat down with a school counselor, and she asked me if I could speak French. I had studied it for three years already and was able to hold a conversation with her. After consulting briefly with my parents, I was put in the French immersion program, one grade higher than I was meant to be.

I'm sure it seemed like a good idea to everyone at the time. My parents also thought it might put some distance between me and the bullying that continued to follow me. But it was a disaster for me socially. I had no friends to speak of during middle school.

There is one illustrative story of failed connection I will share involving yet another school photo. (What is it with me and school photos?) For some reason, it was decided that the theme of our sixth-grade class photo would be twins. It just so happened that there was another Indian girl in that small French immersion class. And of course, there was unanimous agreement among everyone that she and I should be paired together. "It's perfect: you look just like each other!" We looked *nothing* like each other.

I bowed out of attending the eighth-grade graduation party because I didn't want my parents to see I didn't have any friends. Middle school was not an easy time for me by any means.

I opened up somewhat during my high school years, which were an improvement for me over middle school. But I didn't hit my stride or find any real social confidence until the last of my undergraduate years at college. I grew up understanding at a deep and visceral level what it feels like to not belong. And I share these stories with you because I know we have all been there. We all belong to the story of not belonging.

5

LIFE ABROAD

My parents had always wanted to live abroad. Friends who'd had the chance to live for a while in Saudi Arabia, where there are abundant employment opportunities for non-nationals, had raved about the experience. When my father got a job in Saudi, they were excited about the opportunity even though they knew there were some risks involved. They did a lot of research and made our whole family attend cultural sensitivity workshops to prepare us for the move.

We lived in a Canadian compound, where my sister and I attended a prestigious, private international school. It was a stark contrast to the public school in our low- and middle-class neighborhood in Ottawa. The academics at the school were excellent, as was the artistic and athletic programming. But socially we both had trouble navigating this very new, elite environment.

We also encountered a different, in some ways more explicit kind of racism than we'd seen in Canada. It was the first time I'd been called a "Paki" (a derivative of Pakistani, used as a catch-all slur for anyone from Southeast Asia). It was also my introduction to "ref" (for refugee, even though I was anything but), and "FOB" (fresh off the boat).

I experienced racism from not just students but teachers as well. I tried out for the music program and really wanted to play the trumpet. A teacher informed me my lips were too big. When I told my parents, they clearly knew this was wrong. But instead of naming it as racist, they pulled up pictures of countless notable trumpet players—all with big, full lips, and all of whom could play the trumpet just fine, thank you. My parents didn't complain to the school; they didn't address the issue head on. Yet they also weren't going to passively accept this exclusion. When we got back to Canada, they hired me a private trumpet teacher.

While life at the international school was a mixed bag, my parents did take advantage of our proximity both to Asia and to Europe; we traveled, a lot—to India multiple times, to London, to Singapore. I'm sure getting to see so much of the world at a young age informed my worldview.

———

By the time I was a senior in high school, I had been to India many times. When I was in kindergarten, we took six weeks off from school to travel there. There were trips in the second and third grade as well and then more during the year in Saudi. But the trip in high school was under entirely new circumstances. I was in serious danger of not graduating. I needed a wake-up call, and that took the form of spending the balance of my senior year with my aunt's family in India, finishing my high school studies by correspondence. I would have no distractions, no swim competitions, no Indian dance classes. My one and only responsibility was to get my high school degree and get into university.

I remember in particular a talk I had with my father before I left. It turns out he had come to a somewhat similar crossroads early in life himself. My father had been a gifted athlete as a young man and has remained good at sports his entire life. Among other things, he was a promising cricket player. But at a certain point, he had to choose: either stay in India and chase a career in cricket or put school first and come to the US to pursue an MBA. He chose school.

In no uncertain terms, he told me I, too, must choose: school or sports. He drove the point home even deeper. If I didn't start taking my studies seriously, he said, I would end up like Paul Jensen, my swim coach. My parents knew how much I loved Paul, and they appreciated how instrumental his presence had been in my life. They also knew how limited his options were. They didn't want me working a second job at a sporting-goods store.

I got the message and got my act together. There was no social life for me in India that year other than the companionship of my cousin. I finally learned proper study habits—perhaps transferring the discipline I had cultivated in sports.

In India, as in many parts of the world, there is the tradition of the mid-day nap, one I had not developed. So while everyone else slept, I had my one indulgence of TV time, watching music videos on Channel V and staying in touch with what was going on in American pop culture.

I remember watching the Cricket World Cup, the first time my father's old sport had really captured my imagination. I had chosen my studies over sports, but athletics, and the psychology behind them, remained a presence in my life.

6

THE *BEVERLY HILLS 90210* OF ONTARIO

In retrospect, my childhood years formed a solid foundation for the adult I would later evolve in to. I can see how the seeds of my calling were planted early and nurtured by some amazing coaches and teachers. I was blessed to be part of a warm and loving family, and to travel and be exposed to other countries and cultures. Still, in many ways, these were tough years for me. It was a chapter in my life I needed to turn the page on.

I eventually did get into university—if only by a hair. The University of Western Ontario (typically referred to as Western University, or simply Western) is in London, Ontario, a city about half the size of Ottawa. London sits just north of the US-Canadian border a good six hours southwest of Ottawa with Detroit another two hours farther southwest. I got into some schools that were closer, but I needed to put some distance between myself and my home town.

My kinesiology studies were an extension of my athletic life growing up and a manifestation of the critical importance of coaching in my life. I felt this would lead to a line of work where I could help people, perhaps as a physical therapist. Envisioning myself very much in the healthcare field, not in the world of business, I still had the notion that my degree at Western could eventually lead me to medical school.

Although Western has a well-earned reputation as a party school, not everyone, it seems, is invited to the party. Sororities and fraternities dominate social life on campus. Those organizations are almost exclusively white and blonde—to the point where, yes, some call the school the *Beverly Hills 90210* of Ontario. A reputation as a party school usually comes with its share of misogyny and sexual assault. At Western, racism was also prominent in the mix.* I myself did not experience a great deal of overt racism at Western. But it certainly shook up some of my ideas about identity and thus about belonging. There is a fairly prominent Indian community on campus, and (in keeping with the model minority stereotype) I expected them to be quiet and studious. Wrong! They were some of the biggest partiers around.

Not officially part of the school's sorority and fraternity system, WICSA (the Western Indo-Canadian Students Association) often felt like a de facto frat. Their parties were infamous. Unlike in Ottawa—where, through dance class and gatherings hosted by my parents, the local Indian community was a significant part of my life—I never really felt I belonged to the Indian community at Western. Most of my friends were white.

It is perhaps no surprise to you at this point that my tribe turned out to be . . . coaches.

After a difficult time settling into campus life my first year, I applied

---

* The racism on campus, and in London generally, seems to have only gotten worse in the years since I graduated, a dynamic Eternity Martis (who is Black and Pakistani) unpacks in her recent memoir *They Said This Would Be Fun: Race, Campus Life, and Growing Up.*

for a position to mentor incoming freshmen in my second year. (Sound familiar?) The position wasn't paid, but as a perk, I got to live in a single room. My responsibilities grew in subsequent years. In my third year, I was an academic programmer, helping younger students shape their curriculum and study habits. In my fourth year, I was elevated to the position of don, managing the entire residential staff, and was given a room and a salary.

These were my people, my community. At the time, I didn't necessarily view my work mentoring younger students as an experience in leadership development. But that's exactly what it was. And looking back, a couple of challenging situations stand out.

In that third year when I was an academic programmer, I was assigned to a huge residence hall known colloquially as "The Zoo." On a campus known for being a party school, this was one of the most notorious party halls. I would never have chosen to live there in a million years.

There is, of course, a dark side to every party scene: the students who don't fit in, who maybe try to fake it but deep inside are struggling and miserable. Natasha was a first-year student living next to me. I knew she had an eating disorder. What I didn't know was that she had tried to take her life, twice. But when she contemplated a third attempt, she called me. I was trained in listening skills and in talking students through mental health crises, and I guess the training and my natural instincts kicked in. I was able to talk her through it. I can't explain how I managed to maintain my composure and equanimity; the moment felt bigger than both of us. I remained present and attentive. I know that night was a pivotal moment for her, but it was for me too. We are still friends and in touch today.

The second situation involved (not surprisingly) drinking. A party hall we were, but we had rules, and I was in the unenviable position of enforcing them. One of those rules: absolutely no drinking in restrooms and public spaces. During "Frosh Week" (when the partying was at a particularly high pitch), I caught a student, Ruby, doing just that. I had to write her up; she knew I had to do what I had to do, and it wasn't a big deal.

The problem was that a second violation would result in her getting kicked out of the dorm. So she knew she had to be careful and avoid another flagrant violation. But she didn't. A few months later, I caught her doing the same thing.

I didn't just write her up straight away. I went to her and was honest, compassionate, and transparent—and, in a sense, vulnerable. I told her that she had put me in a tough position. I didn't at all relish bringing the hammer down on her. I didn't go to her as an authority figure; I went to her with compassion and empathy, and she responded and shared a lot with me. It wasn't, of course, simply about the drinking. She was dealing with a lot of other things as well. She was apologetic and appreciated my lending her a sympathetic ear.

I was in both an ethical and a strategic bind. If I wrote her up, which I sensed was the right thing to do, everyone on the floor would know it. Yet I couldn't let it slide. Ruby knew the deal—she walked right into it. My decision was unpopular at first. But then a funny thing happened. The floor rallied around me. There were no more violations that year. I had set a tone, and students and fellow advisers alike respected that.

When the don who was supervising me that year recommended me for her position the following year, she cited these two incidents. I was a compassionate listener, and I also wasn't afraid to make a tough call in the moment. I was building a tool kit for business leadership and coaching.

7

THE IVY LEAGUE

All along, I had told my parents (and myself) that phys ed and kinesiology might, in a roundabout and unconventional way, put me on a path to medical school. And the funny thing is, I actually did get into medical school. But I turned it down in favor of studying public health at Yale.

Getting into Yale had always been a dream. Like Western, I barely got in there too. I was first placed on the waiting list; and only after making multiple calls, a visit to campus, and sending (unsolicited) new transcripts and recommendation letters did they finally accept me. (I think I'd exhausted them into admission!) Landing there was a kind of personal redemption for the girl who had flirted with being a high school dropout. I had made it to the Ivy League and was still dancing that delicate dance between playing by the Indian immigrant playbook and testing and resisting it.

In my two years at Yale, and six years at Harvard, my intellectual interests evolved in ways that continue to shape who I am today. And that will indeed be the focus of this chapter. But first: a word about boys.

My late entry into the world of serious dating was partly informed by my cultural upbringing. Another big factor, in retrospect, was my retreat into shyness and introversion as a result of the bullying I experienced. The other turns of fate that caused me to be uncomfortable and socially awkward didn't help, either. It was really only late in my time at Western that I hit my stride and started to feel at home with how I presented to the world. Still, at Western, I got zero interest from boys. It was like I was invisible to them.

It was a very different story at Yale. Almost immediately I had guys asking me out. At the time, I couldn't account for it. Looking back, it's clear to me that this sudden attention was a reflection of my newly found confidence. I was finding my voice. Moving to the States, and Yale in particular, also gave me a blank slate; I could redefine myself and not be at the mercy of the same cultural norms that kept me on the sidelines back in Canada. And being Canadian was, to my American classmates, "cute," which gave me a special and unfamiliar kind of admiration.

Academically, I was slowly but surely finding my sweet spot—although it was hardly a linear path. At Western, I had become fascinated with sports psychology. I was especially struck by the power of visualization: the fact that by simply walking through, in your mind, all of the events leading up to and during a competition, you could significantly improve your performance. It was a testament to the power of mind over body.*

---

* To this day, I regularly incorporate visualization into my work with clients—in particular, exercises where you imagine (and even converse with) your future self. I had a powerful experience of this myself during my coaching training back in 2010. I saw myself in a business suit at the bottom of my stairs, two young children at my heels. Everything was moving quickly, as often happens in dreams, but it was clear I was headed out on a business trip and trying to get on my way while at the same time trying to pay attention to my kids and kiss them goodbye. I "woke" from the visualization feeling surprised (again, a career in business was not the plan) and yet powerfully connected to the scene. Just a few years later, my life played out much this way: with me traveling across the continent, eventually around the world, for coaching and facilitation projects even as my kids were babies.

A deeper dive into psychology was a natural extension of my interest in sports psychology, and a course at Yale in human development was a definite turning point. I began to get a sense of a lens through which to view the world and to understand who we are. That lens didn't fully come into focus until I got to Harvard.

Both academically and socially, my time at Yale was very much a stepping stone, a time of transition. A lot of that was simply a matter of acculturating to the United States and to American culture. There were little things, like knowing what NPR was. Other stark differences between Canada and the US actually were relevant to my studies. There I was, sitting in classes about healthcare, and I couldn't get my head around the fact that people had to research and shop around for and pay for their own private health insurance. I had been living in a Canadian bubble, and it took me a while to learn the ways of what would turn out to be my new home.

———

I ended up at Harvard in part due to an episode that taught me another early lesson about identity and belonging. In a way it echoes my "twin" experience in sixth grade. A professor at Yale encouraged me to apply to PhD programs and made an introduction to a professor at Columbia. She was Indian, and I suppose he assumed (not unreasonably) that she might make a good contact and possible future mentor for me.

The interview and the connection did not pan out, to put it mildly. From the start, she was disparaging and berating. She said I wasn't smart enough to cut it in her program. "You're not going to make it," she told me. "I know your type." (I still don't know what my "type" is.) I distinctly remember her saying to me, "Pack your bags and go."

So I did. For Harvard.

There is an important takeaway here. As I will repeat over and over throughout this book, identity is complicated, multiple, and layered. It is not a single thing. It is not always the most obvious thing. When two people present similarly and appear to have a common ethnic or racial heritage, it is understandable to assume they have much in common. (Like me and the other Indian girl in my sixth-grade class.) They may indeed. But they also may not. Other elements of their identity may make them anything but a good fit.

For example, even as I tried, I never really fit in with the kids who were straight from India; and the Indian-origin kids who were born and raised in North America often denied their Indian roots, which also made it hard for me to relate to them. I learned later, though, that it was only in a truly diverse group that I was able to experience feeling seen and understood. We all find belonging in our own way.

This overarching idea of the complexities and nuances of our identity, and also of our evolution as human beings, made me feel at home intellectually and philosophically at Harvard. Harvard had an entire department called Human Development and Psychology. It was essentially their spin on the field of developmental psychology. The name difference wasn't just semantics. Developmental psych traditionally places a huge emphasis on childhood development, the assumption being that there is this accelerated development happening when we are young that somehow slows or becomes less relevant altogether when we are adults. Harvard had a different take: we are never static; we are constantly growing and evolving. According to this view, everything in front of us is an opportunity for interpretation and learning, and thus for growing. It's like Canadian artist

Alanis Morissette teaches us in her song "You Learn."*

What was falling into place for me was not just an intellectual vision but a life vision. Although I didn't frame it in these terms at the time, I was sensing how the lens of developmental psychology (as I was learning it at Harvard) offers us a kind of grace. It allows us to make mistakes and fail, then learn, repair damage, and try new things. It gives us the chance to develop a vision for ourselves and grow toward it. In other branches of psychology, certain behaviors or modes of thinking are frequently labeled abnormal or pathological. Not so here—in Harvard's framing of developmental psych, you are not wrong for who you are.†

For me, the implications are enormous. This grace creates room to experiment, to be fallible, to be vulnerable—without which we can't grow into our full selves and take on the risky business of inclusive leadership. I can't see the world any differently now.

One professor at Harvard, Marcelo Suárez-Orozco, was a huge influence. He called himself a "psychological anthropologist," and he was studying immigration patterns but very much through a culturally sensitive lens. Marcelo had an acute sense of how culture informs the choices people make and who they are allowed to be. He was relentlessly curious and empathetic in seeking to understand people in the context of their culture.

---

* I had to include a famous Ottawan!
† Other researchers in developmental psych at the time were narrowly steeped in Western notions of development and did not use a cross-cultural perspective. Through that lens, you *could* be wrong for who you are. My human development studies gave a lot of weight to culture and to the importance of being culturally sensitive and humble.

Still, despite Harvard's distinctive take on the field, a more traditional, Western view prevailed much of the time, which is quicker to judge and with a bias toward other cultures and ways of life built in by years of colonialism. I remember a particular proseminar where another student and I were the only two bringing a relativist lens to our work. Everyone else fell back on the Western tradition. It was no coincidence, I think, that the other student, Frank, was Latino and I was Indian. Everyone else in the seminar, with the exception of one Korean, was white.

Marcelo left for NYU in my second year at Harvard, and he actually asked me to follow him. I stayed, but my work with him spilled over into a subsequent connection with Tony Earls, a public health researcher in the medical school (I couldn't seem to stop flirting with medical school). He wasn't grounded intellectually in that same culturally sensitive view, but he appreciated that perspective and welcomed diverse points of view. He eventually became my adviser and invited me to join a big research project he was running in Tanzania.

8

TANZANIA

Tanzania was a formative experience. I took my preparations seriously and spent two years studying Kiswahili before the trip. I was determined not to fall into the trap of the white savior complex. I wanted to understand the culture and the language, and to interact with the population I would be working with—street children who were often members of gangs—on their terms. Speaking Kiswahili was a major advantage in gaining trust. I even collected my data in Kiswahili. Another very particular choice I made once I got there was that there would be no photos of me out in the field. There is simply no getting around the loaded power dynamics and deeply problematic history of white (or in my case lighter-skinned) Westerners working among Africans.

My brown skin was a dilemma for them. They have a word for *white person* that comes in many variations. They weren't quite sure how to place me. "What kind of a *mzungu* [foreigner] are you?" It was another lesson in the nuances of identity, which doesn't conform neatly to the boxes we like to assign to people.

Yet I couldn't escape my power and my privilege, and a fourteen-year-old gang leader reminded me of that one day in a way I will never forget. I was negotiating access to the street children with him. He wanted to know what was in it for him and his people other than the free shoes and lunch I was offering. "You're going to get a book out of this," he told me, "and go back to your comfort and safety and use what you have learned here to advance your career. We get shoes and lunch for a week? What are you going to give us?"

His point was more than fair. Everything he said was true. It was a real moment of reckoning for me. How was I to do this work while remaining true to the culturally sensitive lens I swore by and without falling into Western colonialist trappings? When I got back to Boston, I organized a fundraising drive to provide the rehab center with computers and other support. But beyond that, my research took a significant turn and I delved even deeper into cross-cultural psychology, trying to figure out where my own biases and assumptions came from and how they were hindering my pursuit of deeper connections, knowledge, and relationships.

This was an early lesson in what it means to be an ally—though I didn't think of it at the time.

———

Bob Selman, a psychologist at the School of Education, eventually became my adviser. He supported and believed in me in so many ways. Perhaps the greatest gift he gave to me was a casual observation that he may not have given much thought to at the time.

"Priya, you're good at a lot of things," he said. "You're a talented researcher. But then there's what you do with the students as my teaching assistant. They come in to see you during your open office hours, and they leave feeling on top of the world. I'm not sure exactly what to call what you do with them. It's not teaching. I think it might be coaching. You might think about making a career of it."

A recurrent theme in this book is the tremendous power of naming things. Although doing so has a very particular dynamic in the realm of inclusive leadership, it is effective in all aspects of leadership, coaching, and mentoring. By noting what he felt I was particularly good at, Bob gave a name to something I was not even fully aware I was doing—my style of working one-on-one with students was emerging intuitively, not by design.

Putting a name to something we do and are can limit us, but it can also free us. Bob's observation played an important role in my discovery of my calling. He helped free me to step more fully into myself and my strengths. That's a lot of what good leaders do.

9

THE LIGHTHOUSE GROUP: I JOIN THE TRIBE OF COACHES

Let me get this out of the way: Ultimately, things did not work out for me at LightHouse. I learned a lot and thrived in many ways, but I eventually felt I had to part ways with the company where I grew as a coach and businesswoman. I felt they could have done more with regard to diversity, equity, and inclusion (DEI). Just as important, I believed I could do more to advance that cause by striking out on my own and creating my own company. Also critical in this decision were certain political developments in the country that, in my view and in the view of many, threatened the voices of women, minorities, and other historically excluded groups. I felt a call to act boldly, and I did.

But let me also be clear about this: I hold LightHouse and the people there in extremely high regard. I learned a great deal during my years with them and would not be where I am today if I hadn't been given the opportunity to begin my coaching career there. Yes, I felt their leadership fell short at times, especially when it came to considering diversity and equity. Yet the same could be said for many—if not most—companies, including some of my current clients. We must extend the grace to stumble and be imperfect to organizations as well as individuals. We are all on that same imperfect path to inclusive leadership. We all fall short at times. The important thing is that we learn from our stumbles and stay on the path to learn and do better.

My LightHouse story starts before the company had even been founded. After Harvard, I ended up getting a job at Brandeis as an academic and career counselor. It was a job of convenience, allowing me to be in Boston with my then husband. I was pregnant with my first child, so I wasn't looking to embark on any ambitious ventures. I was good at the job and enjoyed it.

One day, with Bob Selman's words ringing in my ears, I read about a training offered by the Coaches Training Institute (CTI) and asked if Brandeis would be willing to allow me time off to go through the training. It would involve a substantial time commitment: Thursday through Saturday, twice a month. My supervisor felt it would be a good investment and improve my value as an employee, and said sure.

The training was eye-opening for me. If Harvard had been all theory and—aside from the experience in Tanzania—very little in the way of practice, the CTI training was all practice and almost no theory.

I wasn't sure what to make of it all at first. It wasn't so much that I resisted this new approach as that I was in unfamiliar territory. I found myself raising my hand as we were taught a certain practice or skill set and asking questions like: What's the theory behind this? Where is the research establishing this as a best practice?

I was told to stop analyzing, to stop looking to the literature and the theory, and to just be present in the moment. Be present in my own body. Read and respond to what's happening in the room. I went with it and found it unexpectedly liberating.

Academics are sometimes prone to dismiss teachings of the kind that CTI puts forth, precisely because they are not explicitly rooted in theory and formal research. But the practice *is* rooted in research, just research of a different kind: the in-the-moment process of paying attention, being curious, trying things out, noticing what happens, and adjusting.

In a way, that approach is entirely consistent with the core insights of human development that I had fallen in love with in the first place. Our evolution as individuals and communities is fluid and ever-changing; it doesn't proceed along a linear, prescribed, or formulaic path; it is an emergent, organic, living entity.

I also found practical instruction during this training. At Harvard, we learned the *why* of active and compassionate listening. At CTI, we learned the *how*. It turns out there are actual mechanics to the skill set of listening. We weren't given papers or citations to justify these mechanics. Rather, they were simply best practices that had emerged out of the trial and error of coaches working to get better at what they do. They were formulated in the live laboratory of people trying to talk other people through challenging situations.

I soaked it all up. After six months of classroom instruction and then another six months of weekly practical calls, I received my coaching certification in July 2011, the day before I was due to give birth to my first child.

———

I met another woman in that program who would go on to found and be the managing partner of LightHouse Group. We couldn't have been more different. She was in her early forties; I was thirty-two. She came from a very buttoned-up corporate background, having spent years at organizations like the Boston Consulting Group; I was new on the scene. She came to the workshops dressed as any respectable executive would; I showed up in yoga pants.

We didn't really interact much during the six months of our training. But toward the end, she found out that I had two Ivy League masters degrees and a doctorate from Harvard, which surprised her. It turns out she thought I actually *was* a yoga instructor. She approached me about leading an upcoming one-day workshop together, and I agreed. Our styles didn't exactly mesh. It was also clear that she had a great deal more experience than me, and that I could learn a lot from her. But apparently, she saw something in me.

Afterward, she told me she felt we had complementary skill sets and backgrounds. She said she was putting together a team—a "tribe" she called it—and starting her own company. She wanted to know if I was interested.

I was ambivalent. When I ran the offer by my father, he was not in the least ambivalent. "Priya," he said, "she is *handpicking* a select group of people with elite academic backgrounds. You have to do this. You will learn a ton." The Indian immigrant playbook that just hadn't worked for me for years had come back wrapped in new packaging. I had a new opportunity to follow the playbook again, to get back on that track.

He was right. I told her that as long as the birth of my first child in the next couple of months wasn't a problem, I would be happy to join the team.

Almost from the start, I got the sense of not quite fitting in, of being the outsider. I distinctly remember the day we were scheduled to show up at a fancy Boston hotel to have our professional photos taken. (Yes, another story of me and a group photo shoot.) Already, I felt a little out of place. Most of the team was in their fifties. They were all white. Their kids were grown up, and there I was lugging around my four-week-old newborn.

I was nursing Anjali, so she was very much attached to me. I remember feeling like her presence at the photo shoot was seen as an inconvenience. The hotel parking was expensive, and I was unsure as to whether I could or should ask to be reimbursed for it. In short, there was the subtle (but all too familiar) sense of not quite belonging.

Yet there was so much to learn, and I did.

That leader took a huge chance on me and showed great belief in me. I remain enormously grateful to her on both counts.

No, that team of all-white coaches in their fifties wasn't terribly diverse. But they were experienced. Each of them had twenty plus years of experience in the business world and a proven track record. I was a completely green coach coming out of the world of academia. I was an unproven and unknown entity. Yet the leader of the team saw something in me and took a chance on me.

That is something good leaders do. None of us—not the most seasoned leader or any of their top talent—is complete unto ourselves. We have gaps, we have limitations, we have weaknesses, we have deficiencies. We need others with complementary skills and life experiences to round us out and fill in those missing pieces. Good leaders recognize that, and they have an uncanny sense of the right complementary talent to put around them.

(*Spoiler alert:* This is part of why inclusive leaders are better leaders, period. They draw on a larger palette of complementary talent. Their teams are more diverse—not only in terms of demographics but in terms of cognitive style, life experience, and worldview.)

This leader showed she believed in me not just by hiring me in the first place but also by—from the start—giving me choice and challenging assignments. One of those was for one of the largest technology companies in the world. I coached there for years with LightHouse. The experience had its share of ups and downs, and it taught me some valuable lessons.

It was challenging right out of the gate. That company had a scary culture, especially for a relatively green coach. If you weren't careful, they would eat you alive.

In my first session with them, we were in a circle with no tables (already likely departing from what they were used to). My co-facilitator and I began by modeling the process of coaching one another. Usually this initial demonstration is met with at least some interest and curiosity. People will say, "You didn't really solve anything"—problem-solving being at the center of most corporate meetings—"but it's a way of talking that's new and different for us to see." Something like that.

Not here. People immediately began critiquing us. "You seem nervous," they said. "This kind of exercise isn't interesting to us or our company. You should have done your homework."

Group dynamics can be tricky and volatile. Once one person sets a dismissive tone, it grants everyone else permission to do the same. That's exactly what happened. My co-facilitator and I missed an opportunity to dig into that dismissiveness, to interrogate it, to find out what was behind it. I now know, with fifteen additional years of experience under my belt, that would have been the most productive coaching response. Instead, we got defensive. "All right, so how would *you* do it?" We didn't fundamentally challenge them or go deeper. In the end, I took the easy way out—I just gave the client what they wanted.

The man who had set off the barrage of criticism, Carlos, was someone I was coaching one-on-one. It was a missed opportunity for both of us. I should have (and now I most certainly would have) confronted him, even if I chose not to press the issue in front of the group. "What were you thinking? Is that the kind of leader you want to be?" These questions would need to be asked in a tone that was warm and curious not accusing or abrasive. That tone could make all the difference.

Carlos and I had one coaching session where he got real and vulnerable. His mother had just died. He confessed to me that she'd been sick for a while and that he knew he had been a jerk to me. But our coaching relationship never deepened in a lasting way. It wasn't successful or fulfilling for either of us.

I continued to coach at that company for years. In the long run, they became a good client. I had other one-on-one coaching relationships that were more successful. But I knew right away, flying home from that first session, that I needed tougher skin—or at least a different approach. The disappointment, and the missed opportunities, sharpened my skills and my resolve.

10

DANCING IN THE MOMENT

Another early missed opportunity with a different company stands out for me. Another co-facilitator and I, after demonstrating how a coaching conversation works, asked for a volunteer to come up and be coached by the group. Silence. We tried again, talking about the benefits of doing such a session in front of the group and all the things they might get from such an experience.

Still no volunteers. We dropped it, didn't push the issue, and proceeded with our presentation. It wasn't a success. The engagement was low, the feedback likewise, and the client didn't rehire us. This particular co-facilitator and I didn't work together again for a while. And I felt really, really bad—I didn't serve the client, didn't learn anything new, and didn't take any risks. Yuck.

The way I would handle such a situation now (and how I should have handled the disappointment described in the previous chapter) is best captured by a phrase the coaching community loves and repeats often: dancing in the moment. In evolving my own style of coaching, and my own voice as a coach and leader, I have embraced the ethos of that phrase so fully and completely it has taken me outside the standard coaching playbook, beyond where many coaches take it.

A textbook definition of this phrase could be: Coaches are dancing in the moment when they are completely present with the client, holding their client's agenda, accessing their own intuition, and letting the client lead them. When coaches dance in the moment, they are open to any steps the client takes and are willing to go in the client's direction and flow.

I interpret this phrase a bit differently. I don't always defer to the client's agenda and lead. At times, I push, challenge, and confront—with empathy and compassion, but with a directness and candor that sometimes creates initial discomfort. The way, say, Paul Jensen or Pansy Lin would have.

I am also more direct than many coaches in sharing my own feelings and state of mind, my own experience and how it's playing out in the space between us, and my own vulnerability. I call this technique "sharing my process." If I had a do-over at that technology company, for example, I would share openly how their critique made me feel. I would follow that up by saying, "I feel dismissed and wrongfully accused by your statements. What is behind your impulse to talk to us in this way?"

Though this approach—which I now take more often than not—may sound direct and tough, my candor is paired with concern, warmth, and even empathy in my tone and in my intent. My aim is to connect, not to win a contest of wills. Most of the time, this kind of sharing and vulnerability are met with reciprocity—because to reciprocate is a normal human impulse. People respond in kind and open up. These initially uncomfortable moments are often when the magic happens.

It's not about my feelings and making it personal. I am modeling vulnerability. I am also modeling how to name things in a productive way. The objective is to name the feeling or thought—often the unsaid or uncomfortable one—and then frame it in a way so as to get at the larger issue at play. To get at the elephant in the room. In this way, I also model the kind of truth-telling and sharing I expect of my clients and myself.

My objective is the same when I'm pressing an issue or challenging a client. The point is to draw out the latent discomfort, to take what is unsaid and sitting below the waterline and bring it to the surface. To me, that process of digging, inquiring, challenging, and getting curious is what dancing in the moment is all about. There is tremendous untapped power and latent energy in what is not said, in what people feel they can't say. There is, as well, power in being frank and candid about what's going on internally. All of that is alive in the room and is the raw material that coaches, and leaders, can and should make use of. It is, I think, the nuts and bolts of "inclusive" dialogue. A good leader includes what is being said *and* what is not being said, and they create space for all of it, knowing there is wisdom and greater learning in all those moments.

What's funny is even though I missed a couple of early opportunities to dance in the moment at LightHouse, I had already begun tapping into my native instincts and discovering my style and voice during my training with CTI. In those sessions, we did a lot of role-playing that anticipated exactly the kind of coaching demonstrations I have just described. When I volunteered to coach a "client" in front of the class, I found I had a knack for cutting to the chase—for asking the kind of frank and direct questions that would stop people in their tracks.

As I settled in and became more confident at LightHouse, I started to see more of that as well. When a client would say, "I've never heard myself speak this way," it felt gratifying and rewarding. I wanted to explore it more.

11

GOING OFF SCRIPT

In stark contrast to those fumbled experiences, I had a different extended coaching assignment that went swimmingly. There, with the help of an extremely supportive and collaborative colleague, I was able to carve out the freedom to explore my own style of coaching.

LightHouse had developed another offering where we worked with a group of leaders and taught them how to coach one another. I was paired with another facilitator, Mark, to do the training at a midsized health-technology company.

The leadership at LightHouse had a very clear idea of the material and how they wanted it to be presented. The entire training was tightly scripted. For the first half of the day, Mark and I stuck to the script. Over lunch we compared notes and realized, while it seemed to be going well, neither of us was having fun. The script wasn't demanding, nor did it allow any creativity on our part. "Let's go off script," we said to one another at our lunch break.

We realized we were taking a chance. We understood that LightHouse might not be happy if word got back to them. But we had to follow our instincts. And both of us were empowered by knowing that we had a willing coconspirator.

In our afternoon sessions, we went wildly off script. With my group, I danced in the moment, taught new skills that I'd never before rehearsed, gave feedback, challenged assumptions, and shared my process—loudly and unabashedly. I felt invigorated. The participants loved the idea of "throwing away the agenda" and, in turn, said they were going to try that with their teams. They felt energized to be creative in the moment rather than to follow a script. When I met up with Mark at the end of the day over a glass of wine, he had a similar experience. He shared, "We need to do *that* more often."

The risk paid off. We got great feedback scores, the client loved the training, and they purchased the package for other teams at other branches. They became one of our best repeat customers. Soon Mark and I were flying around the country replicating that training and refining it. I don't think I've ever met someone else who lived and breathed coaching like Mark did. And who was so doggedly committed to continually refining (and redefining) the craft.

The leadership at LightHouse knew we had captured some magic, and they wanted to spread that magic around. The leadership team had us demonstrate our training to the rest of the LightHouse facilitators. It was a tricky moment because the cat was definitely out of the bag at that point. When we revealed that, for the most part, we didn't rely on a script, many of the other coaches were flabbergasted; we had been conditioned to do as we were told. The leadership team, for their part, didn't criticize us. They framed it diplomatically—and, interestingly, in terms of diversity. "Coaches bring different personalities and different cognitive styles to their work," they said. Some people felt they worked best with a script. But for others, a script might just be a jumping off point.

While the leader of LightHouse was receptive to our contrasting approach, she chose, for whatever reason, to break Mark and me up. Maybe she thought we could replicate our success with other partners.

It didn't happen. The feedback scores dropped considerably after that. I continued to push the boundaries on my own but never found such a like-minded partner at LightHouse.

Although it didn't last, that partnership with Mark was enormously formative. I realized that, for me, the only way to fully dance in the moment *was* to go off script. It forces you to be radically present in the moment. You can't afford to go on autopilot. Your authentic voice rises to the surface, and that can be scary. So is the very real possibility that, in tightrope walking without a net, you will make mistakes. But when you take that risk, others, sensing that, feel they have permission to take risks as well.

I remember thinking at the time, *I want to be part of a company where* everyone *gets to be the coach they* mean *to be.*

12

SPEAKING UP

I was finding my way and developing my own style at LightHouse. I generally got good feedback from clients and the leadership team. But apart from that experience with Mark, I was also playing it safe and biding my time in a way that is not atypical for immigrants or people of color in the corporate world. In Mark, I had an ally; I wouldn't get my wrists slapped because we were in it together, and he supported me. But like my parents before me, I sensed I was on foreign soil. I didn't want to make a critical misstep, so I chose not to rock the boat, even when something didn't sit right with me. I would pay my dues and be a good team player until I had more equity, more standing, more leverage.

Those decisions—to bide your time and bite your tongue—are so common for immigrants, people of color, and other underrepresented groups. So is the feeling that you have to go above and beyond; that you have to not just match but exceed the work and hustle of your white male counterparts in order to establish yourself.

So for years I kept my head down and worked. Until one day when everything changed.

LightHouse has a retreat every year to give us space (as is the practice for many companies and organizations) to reflect on our mission and values. The LightHouse retreat involves an exercise called "the fish-bowl" where the leadership team sits in the center and articulates where the company is and where it's headed. Everyone else sits around them and then comments at the end.

I had been cognizant of the fact that LightHouse had a diversity problem. I had been doing the time and waiting for the right moment to confront the issue head on. As the discussion after the fishbowl ran on, I realized this was it; I could hold my tongue no longer.

I didn't exactly jump in. I waited, hoping someone else would raise the issue. It seemed so glaringly obvious. Yet people were saying things like, "Wow, the leadership team has really been thoughtful about our offerings," or, "I didn't realize that Keynotes would also be another part of our services, and we should feature those more prominently." Valid, granular issues—but not the elephant in the room that seemed so obvious to me. Couldn't others sense it?

Finally I spoke up. "The entire leadership team is straight, white, middle-aged women. I am the only person of color in the room. Is this not an issue we need to deal with?"

There was silence at first, awkward silence. Then, people started speaking. They were polite, not defensive. People thanked me for showing the courage to speak up. Some said, "Yes, yes, I was going to mention it; I'm glad you did. Yes, this is something we need to address."

On one hand, there was a kind of receptiveness to what I had said. And a genuine show of concern for me, and even admiration for what I had done. But the discussion quickly revealed itself to be a smaller and narrower conversation than the one I had hoped to inspire.

When someone brings up racism or privilege or bias, then challenges a group to examine what it is doing or not doing to address these issues, that challenge is often met with an attempt to deflect. These are difficult issues. It is not easy to look oneself in the mirror and admit to coming up short. But leadership is about tough conversations. Unfortunately, people (even well-intentioned people) are good at avoiding those conversations when it comes to race, privilege, and bias.

Sometimes that deflection takes the form of obvious resistance or defensiveness. It did not in this case. The deflection was more subtle. Instead of examining the company's limitations and the paths the leadership had not chosen, it became about me. First, about my feelings. People wanted to know what they could do to make me feel better. I didn't want to talk about my feelings. When failings around diversity become about an individual's feelings, then the response veers in the direction of an apology instead of toward a larger effort to course correct and truly understand the roots of the issue. They should've been focused on why LightHouse was an all-white group with just one person of color in the first place.

I also became tokenized. I became LightHouse's face and voice for underrepresented minorities. There was an attempt afterward to make our recruiting more diverse. But it was assumed that I should be the go-to person to interview them. When a client needed a more "diverse" coach, I was, again, the go-to person.

This is a common and problematic pattern in the corporate world. When—in response to an internal crisis, George Floyd, or something else—an organization decides to get serious about diversity, it is assumed that people of color or other historically underrepresented identities on staff will want to bear a disproportionate burden of any new diversity initiative. They may indeed want to step up. Often, however, and for very good reasons, they will not want that additional burden. In my case, I was happy to be part of the solution, but I didn't want to be the point person. I didn't feel that was my job.

Yet for better or worse (or a bit of both), that incident at the retreat *became* my identity at the company. I couldn't shake it. In a sense I was typecast. I was approached with questions like, "What's it like to be brown?" (I don't know—what's it like to be white?)

Some of those ripple effects were positive. To this day, I still learn about people who heard of the incident and were inspired to speak up.

I was glad I'd spoken up. But I found myself in a box. I knew I had to get out.

13

BREAKING THROUGH RESISTANCE

I had essentially become the voice of DEI at LightHouse. But in my bones, I knew that wasn't the right path for me. Not now. I knew it was time to make good on the promise I'd made to myself during those formative and freeing trainings with Mark: to found and build a company where off-script, authentic coaching and leading could be the norm and not the exception.

So much more was at stake during this time than my personal vision for coaching. The day after the US presidential election of 2016, as though waking up to a nightmare world in which the voices of women and minorities would be categorically dismissed and minimized, I registered the name RoundTable and began putting together the pieces to start my own company. I felt ready to go off on my own but wasn't quite sure what that was going to look like. I trusted in myself and in my vision—which was simple: to inspire and support people in being who they know they are meant to be.

This vision and wording were inspired by Dr. Dolly Chugh's book *The Person You Mean to Be.*[*] I was deeply compelled by her notion that most

---

[*] Dolly Chugh, *The Person You Mean to Be: How Good People Fight Bias* (New York: Harper Business, 2018).

of us believe we are good people, that we are not as biased or prejudiced as others. But we can't fully escape the reality of cognitive and unconscious biases that can thwart even our best intentions to do good and be good people in the world. What we need to do is recognize our fallibility, be willing to learn, and persist even when it's hard.

When I accepted my own imperfections, thanks to her book, it felt like I'd reached a new kind of freedom. I could lead, inspire, and live better. I wanted to let others in on that fundamental secret of leadership, and I felt that I finally knew how: through courageous conversations, radical acceptance of self and others, and broadening perspectives.

In naming the company, I instinctively reached back to the memory of the two flawed but wonderfully welcoming tables of my parents, around which so much of our family and extended family life had happened. They were spaces of belonging, celebration, learning, creating, tension, and collaboration. There was always a seat at those tables—for anyone. And I wanted to extend that same promise to my company and the broader business world.

———

I have been humbled and fortified by the rapid growth of RoundTable. Perhaps even more so by the fact that the ideas and mission we stand for seem to resonate with so many people. I have been inspired by the courage, compassion, and empathy I have witnessed in my clients as they grow (and stumble) on the journey to being more inclusive leaders.

I have also, I must point out, witnessed resistance. These points of resistance are yet another stumble in our collective journey toward greater inclusion. We must not be disheartened by them. They have much to teach us about our flawed nature as human beings and about how deeply entrenched and often intransigent are the systems and cultures of bias and privilege we seek to change. But we must also be fierce and stubborn in the face of such resistance. We must call it out and name it for what it is—and yet do so in a way that is useful, in a way that can be grasped, in a way that will lead to change.

Sometimes, resistance shows up as inflection points where leaders who seem wholly committed to diversity, equity, and inclusion come to a critical juncture—often a particularly vexing challenge—and suddenly inclusion becomes . . . not so much *not* a priority as an expendable one. One that can be superseded or overridden by another more pressing priority.

People of color, women, and other historically excluded people inevitably encounter resistance in spaces of power as they seek to find their voice and claim their ground. I encountered this type of resistance in the form of a legal tussle with a former employer, which eventually ended in my favor. The details aren't important to go into here. What is important is the larger truth that some resist welcoming people into a space they felt was "theirs."

These two types of resistance are intimately connected. I look back at the way my parents at times muted their public voices and how they did so out of a caution borne of feeling they were treading on foreign territory, on soil not fully their own. Such is the case for so many immigrants, women, LGBTQIA+ and TGNC people, and people of color as they try to find their way in realms traditionally dominated by straight white men. This is why our initial strategy is often to put our heads down, bite our tongues, and work above and beyond in an effort to "prove ourselves" or "pay our dues."

At some point, however, we find we can stay silent no longer. When we make that stand, we are in a sense planting a flag in the ground and claiming the soil beneath us—and on which we might once have felt we walked as outsiders—as our own. To find our voice we must stand our ground, and to stand our ground we must first claim it.

When we do so, we will often meet resistance. At times from those who appear to be our allies. I repeatedly see stories of women of color (these are the ones that jump out at me) in the corporate world who are empowered to speak up and advocate for change—and then punished for doing so.

Overcoming that resistance—and, for allies, recognizing that resistance and calling it out—is an important battle in the campaign for a more inclusive world.

In my legal case, I successfully stood my ground. When I was able to put the matter behind me, when there were no clouds hanging over that flag I had planted in the ground, that was when RoundTable really took off. A key client who had purchased the JEDI© (justice, equity, diversity, and inclusion) training package for his leadership team decided to expand the training to his whole company. Soon after, a second client did the same. I had to scramble to hire and onboard enough facilitators to keep up with business. It was a nice problem to have.

14

MY STORY, OUR STORY

A few things surprised me as I dug deeper into my own narrative in order to write this book. Or maybe in some cases, it's not so much that I was surprised as that certain themes in my life took on new clarity and new gravity once I had named them and taken the time to flesh them out on the page. As I've already indicated, a core tenet of mine is that the act of naming is a powerful one.

I realize now that my parents departed from the Indian immigrant narrative in ways I perhaps did not appreciate or give them credit for at the time. They established themselves firmly in their adopted homeland of Canada and in our tight Ottawa neighborhood of Crystal Beach. Then they became, in their own fashion, globetrotters, traveling from Saudi Arabia to Europe and to the UK. They gave up a life that they had built, one that was familiar and comfortable, in order to create a better life for their children. There was a cost to the chances and choices they took. This, in essence, is a classic immigrant experience. Marcelo, my former professor at Harvard, talks about how migration decisions are often motivated by the promise of "becoming somebody." Such was the case for my parents.

On some level, my father realized the model minority ideal, but he was also held back and constrained by his minority status. I should also acknowledge that my father was a strong voice for women at his company and consistently elevated the women around him. So I had an early role model for what it meant to be an inclusive leader. Ironically, my father was forced into early retirement (as were many other men of color at the company) in the wake of an initiative to increase the ranks of women in leadership positions. He and my mother returned to Saudi Arabia, and he was later sought after by recruiters in Europe. Thankfully, these ended up being some of the best years of his career.

I am also struck and deeply moved by my mother's role in shaping my narrative. The story of that fateful day in a kindergarten gymnasium is as much hers as it is mine. We like to think we are the sole and exclusive authors of our own stories. But in fact we have numerous coauthors and collaborators. The collective family stories (just to cite one group of coauthors) that form so much of our personal mythologies—stories told over and over, which, perhaps, morph over time and vary according to the occasion and the teller—are hardly ours alone.

Then, there is Mrs. Haley (from the story I opened part I with), who spoke up for me at a time when I was in no position to speak for myself. At that point in our young development, our inner voice is very much a work in progress. It is in many ways an amalgam, a mixtape of the outside voices that define our world—and to a large extent our worldview. I honestly can't retrieve my innermost thoughts from that day. But I know that if I could, Mrs. Haley's kind voice would be prominent in the mix.

She was kind, but she went beyond merely being kind and welcoming me into the fold. She chose to address her remarks to Sebastian, who she must have recognized as a bully in the making, troubled and fighting his own demons. Her words were addressed to all of us, and certainly to me. But in an act that was both kind and remarkably skillful—I must credit her, too, as an early model of inclusive leadership—her invitation of welcome and belonging was extended first and foremost to the one who had attempted to exclude. "Isn't it nice that we get to sit here together?"

Our stories are not entirely ours alone. And neither are our voices.

PART II

THE IMPORTANCE OF INCLUSIVE LEADERSHIP

15

SYSTEMS ARE STUBBORN

Our personal stories and voices are not ours alone; they're inseparable from the networks and communities that help define our
identity.

This holds true for larger stories about identity, belonging, and privilege as well. These narratives, and how we think and talk about them, are
shaped by ripples of connection that cross individuals and communities
and continents—and years and decades and centuries.

That vast canvas of humanity and time can overwhelm and daunt us.
It can make us feel small and insignificant. So when we talk about difficult
issues like racism, we may be tempted to particularize and personalize.
If you are white and the issue of reparations comes up, you may think to
yourself, *My ancestors weren't slaveholders. And if they were, it wasn't a
choice I made.* Or you may feel a stab of defensiveness when a term like
white supremacy is used. *Are you saying that I personally am a racist?*

Part of your pushback may be a sense that a term like *systemic racism*
glosses over the differences among individuals in a given system, it
lacks nuance. And you would be right, up to a point. Yet the power and
insidiousness of broader patterns of privilege and bias is that they often
transcend individual choice and intention. They have, you might say, a

mind and will of their own. They have tremendous reach. And they are extremely resistant to change.

HEALTHCARE

By way of illustration, let's briefly look at a few examples of how hard it is to change deeply entrenched systemic bias and inequality and the systems of belief that support them. The first is drawn from *The Color of Care*, a powerful documentary produced by Oprah Winfrey about how long-standing racial inequities in the American healthcare system were both revealed and amplified during the global COVID-19 pandemic.

Disparities in the treatment of kidney disease are one potent case in point. Black Americans are two to four times more likely to suffer from advanced kidney disease—and yet are far less likely to be recommended for a transplant (the most effective treatment). They will stay on dialysis (the inferior treatment) longer and spend more time on transplant waiting lists. A doctor interviewed in the documentary breaks down one reason why this may be the case. The Institutes of Medicine has found that white doctors spend less time explaining complex procedures to their Black patients. They quite possibly assume a Black patient can't afford the procedure, wouldn't understand it, or wouldn't follow through on the pre-scribed post-op care protocol. So, on average, they are less likely to be designated as good candidates for a kidney transplant.

Are doctors consciously discriminating against Black patients? I'd like to believe they are not, for the most part. Yet their "clinical intuition" remains vulnerable to deeply entrenched historical bias.

GENERATIONAL WEALTH

Another example is a stubborn pattern of racialized economic inequality in the United States, both as measured by income and total wealth. Greater wealth parity is a particularly elusive goal because wealth accumulation (our fascination with sudden success stories notwithstanding) tends to be a gradual, intergenerational process. Think of it as a relay race, with each generation handing off the baton to the next, each building on past progress and momentum. Except that Black families in America are starting that relay race late, already a lap or two behind and carrying the weight of ongoing discrimination as they seek to catch up.

This is not ancient history. Many American families entered the middle class during the post-WWII economic boom when the federal government provided massive subsidies to promote expanded homeownership, the foundation for economic security for many families. But most Black families were locked out of that opportunity by redlining and other discriminatory practices in the real estate industry. Those disparities continue to the present day. After a decade in which all forms of inequality have grown, the rate of Black homeownership remains essentially what it was when the United States Fair Housing Act was passed in 1968.

CORPORATE LEADERSHIP

A final example from the corporate world: the representation of Black women at the executive level remains dismal despite a lot of talk and many recent initiatives around DEI. While the lack of a talent "pipeline" is often blamed, a good deal of progress has been made at the entry level. But there is a huge drop-off for Black women as they seek to rise up the corporate ladder—far steeper than the drop-off for women in general (which is bad enough).

While women constitute 48 percent of entry-level employees, they make up only 24 percent of C-suite leadership; for Black women, those numbers are 17 percent and 4 percent respectively. The latter figure in particular has been stubbornly resistant to change.

The 2022 *Women in the Workplace* report by McKinsey & Company and LeanIn.org suggests one explanation. While considerable attention has been paid to the problem of bias in interviews, there has been little scrutiny of bias in performance reviews.[*]

---

[*] LeanIn.org and McKinsey & Company, *Women in the Workplace 2022* report, https://www.mckinsey.com/featured-insights/diversity-and-inclusion/women-in-the-workplace.

16

VOCABULARY

Language is part of culture and is essential to our individual consciousness, our individual psychology. We think of the language constantly streaming through us as our own—the thoughts or feelings we express to others, or simply the running inner dialogue that follows us wherever we go. But is it? We can—to an extent—put our own spin on it. Yet we inherit so many received definitions and understandings starting at an age when we are so impressionable. How much choice, how much agency, do we have in the matter?

From the start, language is a social activity. At an early age, it is between us and our parents, siblings, and larger family; later, with teachers and peers at school; and gradually, among the larger society. Meaning is always active and social and in the space between people. None of us can claim sole possession of it.

Although we are comforted by the seeming certainty offered by the dictionary with its fixed definitions, the meaning of words and phrases is fluid and constantly changing. Definitions are an imperfect attempt to hit a moving target.

But we must do our best with the imperfect language we have. And in a conversation about such challenging matters as bias and privilege, it helps to try to define the terms of that conversation at the outset. We need these terms because they help us understand and talk about how inclusive leadership plays out in the world of work. We just shouldn't expect too much of this language.

The vocabulary of inclusion is imperfect, fluid, and constantly changing. The language with which we talk about inclusion is inherently problematic in every sense of the word. It is intimately tied up with social, cultural, and political conflict over how to resolve long-standing problems of inequity. If the issue at hand presents enormous difficulties, why shouldn't we expect the language to be a problem as well?

As I define frequently used terms in the conversation around inclusive leadership, some of those terms are contested or problematic. I must acknowledge that and explain why. Ultimately, I've tried to find common ground.

SPECIFIC LANGUAGE ABOUT DIFFERENCE

Before we get into working definitions for some of the terms that will come up later in this book, and in most conversations around inclusion, let's take a quick look at the uneasy history of some of the language we use to talk about difference.

Black Americans were first called Negros (and of course, far worse). Then colored, then black, then Black, then African American. In recent years, *person of color* has come into usage. (Some impatient with the fluid and evolving nature of this language might quip, "But I thought we weren't supposed to call you *colored* anymore!" It's not the same.) BIPOC (Black, Indigenous, People of Color) is a more recent evolution. And so on.

———

The vocabulary around gender and sexuality has traveled an even more complicated path in recent decades. In fact, even the language for describing this broad unwieldy category is complicated. Some use SOGI (sexual orientation, gender identity) while others use SOGIE (sexual orientation, gender identity, and gender expression). Yes, gender expression is different from gender identity. Yes, it's complicated.

We used to label people who aren't heterosexual as homosexual—a term seen as clinical and as defining people solely in terms of sexual attraction. *Gay* and *straight* eventually became the dominant terms for describing sexual orientation (although some gay women prefer *lesbian*). *Queer* captures the fluid identity of those who don't want to be narrowly pigeonholed. *Nonbinary* evokes a similar fluidity in gender identity or gender expression. We've all grown familiar with the acronym LGBT (lesbian, gay, bisexual, transgender), which continues to evolve—some now prefer the more broadly inclusive LGBTQIA+ (lesbian, gay, bisexual, transgender, queer/questioning, intersex, asexual/agender). And more recently, TGNC is the acronym we use for the transgender nonconforming community.

It can all be challenging to keep up with. But dismissive questions like, "How many letters do we need?" don't help matters. (The answer: probably as many as it takes. We used to think of gender and sexuality as a binary either/or. We now know this is not the case.)

———

One final example concerns the language used in America to refer to people whose heritage hails from Spanish-speaking countries. For a while, variations of *Spanish-speaking* were used to describe this incredibly diverse group of peoples and histories. In 1980, the US Census formally introduced the term *Hispanic*—which has remained a part of the vocabulary but also has serious limitations. It derives from *Hispania* (Iberian Peninsula, Spain), and so centers and gives primacy to the colonizer and not the independent countries and cultures that eventually came to be. *Latino* has emerged for some as a more inclusive alternative (embracing the entire Latin American experience, including Brazil). Other terms like *Chicano* have entered the lexicon that more closely identify with particular countries or regions.

Latinx (Latin-ex) is a relatively new term around which there has been a great deal of hand-wringing. In that term we see our last two conversations intersect: According to some, it is an attempt to come up with a gender-neutral, nonbinary way to resolve the fixed binary choice of Latino (masculine) or Latina (feminine). Critics argue that it is an artificial and cumbersome term. Defenders say it is not meant to be a definitive term—just a way to open the door to those who may have felt excluded by previous language.

The language we use to talk about Asian Americans has also shifted. It is hard to believe that the term *Orientals* was once widely in use. And as with any term which casts a wide net in trying to capture the historical experience of a large group of people, *Asian Americans* has its problems. People may not initially think of those of Indian heritage as Asian, but the Indian subcontinent—which includes India, Pakistan, Sri Lanka, Nepal, and others—is indeed a region of Asia.

———

I hope these brief (and greatly simplified!) histories give you a sense that when the vocabulary around DEI seems to be shifting before your very eyes—in ways that might confuse you or even make you uncomfortable—it is not someone deliberately trying to confound you. Nor is it someone going out of their way to be "woke" or "politically correct." No, the impetus for change comes, almost always, from someone who does not feel embraced or accepted by the current language. It is really that simple. It is about the basic human need to be included.

GLOSSARY

With all that said, here is a short glossary of some terms that I use in my trainings and that invariably come up in discussions of diversity and inclusion. I have grouped these terms by theme rather than setting them in alphabetical order. I hope this helps better illuminate the relationships between these ideas and makes the definitions easier to understand.

These definitions are not meant to be definitive. They are works-in-progress in an evolving and fluid conversation. But they are a necessary starting point. As a guide put out by the Annie E. Casey Foundation puts it, to illuminate racism, we need to "name it, frame it and explain it."*

Race: Categories based on physical characteristics such as skin color, hair type, facial form, and eye shape. Once thought of as a biological category, race is now widely seen as a social construct.

Racism: The marginalization and/or oppression of people of color based on a socially constructed racial hierarchy that privileges white people.

---

* Annie E. Casey Foundation, *Race Equity and Inclusion Action Guide: 7 Steps to Advance and Embed Race Equity and Inclusion Within Your Organization*, 2014, https://assets.aecf.org/m/resourcedoc/AECF_EmbracingEquity7Steps-2014.pdf.

Larger than personal prejudice, racism is in fact a complex system of hierarchies and inequities.

Systemic Racism: A combination of systems, institutions, and factors that advantage white people and, for people of color, cause widespread harm and disadvantages in access and opportunity. It is grounded in institutions and laws, and expressed in culture and interpersonal behavior.

White Supremacy: Not necessarily an explicit ideology of racial supremacy and inferiority. Rather, it is the more subtle systematic marginalization or oppression of people of color based on a socially constructed racial hierarchy that privileges people who identify as white, regardless of the conscious intent of any one individual.

Microaggressions: The daily slights, comments, remarks, and gestures that communicate exclusion, difference, and discrimination. Micro-aggressions may seem small and come off as jokes. Often there is no conscious ill intent behind them. But the damage they cause is real. The message behind them is simple: you are identity X—therefore I assume Y about you. That kind of reductionist thinking strips a person of their full humanity. In the workplace, microaggressions also often involve subtle ways of being dismissed or cut off in meetings.

Equality: A focus on sameness of treatment and the removal of barriers.

Equity: Supplements the ideal of equality by acknowledging that, because of historical disadvantages, sameness of treatment may not translate into real equality of opportunity. Affirmative action is an example of an equity initiative.

Racial Equity Lens: A set of questions we can ask ourselves as part of a thoughtful and deliberate decision-making process. Comparable to an environmental impact review, the idea is to prevent the unintended consequences of major decisions on diversity, inclusion, and equity—impacts that would not be detected in a "race-neutral" review.

Cultural Competence: The ability to understand, appreciate, and interact with people from cultures or belief systems different from one's own. If implicit-bias training is the management of unconscious bias, cultural-competence training is the positive cultivation of a greater understanding and appreciation of diverse cultures and identities.

Cultural Humility: If cultural competence is about mastery, then cultural humility is about learning. As I will discuss in greater detail later, it is an awareness of one's limitations in understanding anyone's cultural background and experience, and an ongoing commitment to examine and question one's assumptions and biases.

Cultural Sensitivity: Being aware that cultural differences and similarities between people exist without assigning judgment or value to those differences and similarities.

Patriarchy: Narrowly, a society in which the father or eldest male is the head of the family, and where descent is traced through the male line. More broadly, a society in which men have more advantages and everyone else faces more disadvantages. A historical creation in which the fluid and complementary gender roles of hunter-gatherers became rigid and hierarchical.

Neurodivergent: A recognition of the fact that some people's brain's functions, behaviors, and processes are different from what is considered standard (or neurotypical). People on the autism spectrum are one example.

Social Identity Group: A person's sense of who they are based on their membership in a certain group or groups. These groups are united and defined by common characteristics such as language, culture, race, and gender. The common ground can also be things like school, a neighborhood, a baseball team, a political party, etc. We all have multiple identities.

Target: Social identity groups that are oppressed, disenfranchised, subordinated, exploited, and/or otherwise harmed.

Agent: Members of dominant social groups privileged by birth or acquisition who knowingly or unknowingly reap or exploit unfair advantages over members of the target groups.

Headwinds: The unearned and undeserved disadvantages and hardships people face because of a socially defined hierarchy of social-identity groupings.

Tailwinds: The unearned and undeserved advantages, opportunities, and resources that people get by identifying with certain social-identity groups.

Minority: A kind of catch-all for who is *not* in the dominant/majority group. But it can be a euphemism for talking about race and ethnicity. It can come across as dismissive as well, characterizing an entire group or culture exclusively in terms of its relationship to the majority. *Historically underrepresented* is more commonly used now.

Diversity, Equity, and Inclusion

Someone new to this topic might wonder, "Why do we need three terms? Isn't *diversity* sufficient?" These terms—whether used separately or in tandem—are a good marker of how our thinking on this topic has evolved and will continue to do so.

Two decades ago, an inclusive leader at a company might have been designated their chief diversity officer, and that term is still widely used. But diversity alone is strictly a numbers game. Numbers are certainly part of the picture, and setting hiring targets around gender and race helps track progress. But what the *Harvard Business Review* calls an "add diversity and stir" approach doesn't get you very far.* Women and people of color may be in the room but may not feel they have an equal place at the table. There is the danger of tokenism.

One way to put it is that diversity creates a potential to be tapped; you need equity and inclusion to fully harness and leverage that potential. Those two things involve changing business as usual, shifting the power structure and culture.

Equity means there is an active effort to right past wrongs. It acknowledges that "equal treatment" is insufficient given historical inequities and ongoing disadvantages faced by different groups.

Inclusion means a diverse group of people are not just in the room but feel understood and accepted. They feel they belong. (*Belonging* is such a powerful idea that some have added it to DEI.)

---

* Robin Ely and David A. Thomas, "Getting Serious about Diversity: Enough Already with the Business Case," *Harvard Business Review* 98, no. 6 (November-December 2020): 114–122.

Justice: The quality of being just, impartial, or fair. That's the dictionary definition.

But the reason it comes first in JEDI© (and last but not least in our brief glossary here) is not primarily because it makes for a catchy acronym. On the one hand, I like to make it clear that our objective is not to change the world but to change individual workplaces and individuals. On the other hand, larger struggles in society provide important context. The very language we use in DEI work is often borne out of political movements where people organize and agitate for change. Those larger struggles are ongoing and continue to inform, test, and challenge what we do in the workplace. Inclusive leaders need to be cognizant of—and to some extent in dialogue with—that bigger context.

Once again, the murder of George Floyd was a watershed moment. Business leaders realized they couldn't just ignore it and talk about this month's sales goals. They had to create space for conversations that in a narrow sense had nothing to do with work, but that were essential nonetheless. In a very different way, the pandemic also shattered artificial divisions between what was and was not "work-related."

———

Let me say, in closing, I am keenly aware of how charged and politicized (and potentially divisive) language gets when we talk about diversity and inclusion and volatile topics like sexism and racism. We cannot hope to escape or transcend those politics. But when you encounter unfamiliar or challenging language around DEI, try to step back from politics. Get curious. Focus on the human experience. Behind each evolution in language is, more than anything, a group of people—and their pain from not experiencing being an important part of the whole—who want to be included and understood.

I encourage you to be intentional and respectful in your use of language. And yet *not* so careful as to become stuck with the fear of saying the wrong thing. (I see this happen, a lot.) Extend to yourself and others the grace to stumble with your words, the permission to be unsure of how to say something, and the encouragement to go ahead and give it your best try anyway.

View the friction over language as data. What is beneath a disconnect over language? What am I not seeing? Who is not being included? In what ways are people not listening to one another?

> ### David Sedaris Doesn't Want to Be Queer Anymore
> David Sedaris is an author and humorist who first caught the public's attention through his droll, sharply observed stories on National Public Radio's *This American Life*. He is that rare author who can fill and sell out an auditorium wherever he goes. And he's gay, which he's fine with. But now, suddenly, he doesn't want to be known as queer.
>
> In an oddly unfunny, unoriginal commentary on the CBS *Sunday Morning* show, Sedaris complains about having to "rebrand for the fourth time."* First he was homosexual, then

---

* David Sedaris, "David Sedaris on Coming Out, All Over Again," CBS News, October, 16, 2022, https://www.cbsnews.com/video/david-sedaris-on-coming-out-all-over-again/.

gay, then LGBT, and now—suddenly, he says—he has to adopt the moniker of queer.

Never mind the fact that *queer* (originally a slur) has been embraced by gay activists for decades, if not longer. What's disappointing about Sedaris's rant is that it leans on the same tired complaints about the evolving language of identity. We talked earlier about how much our language has evolved in, for example, talking about African Americans. Sedaris sounds a little like an exasperated white person saying to a Black person, "I thought you didn't like being called *colored*. But now we're supposed to call you *people of color*?"

There's no "supposed to" here, and that's a big thing Sedaris gets wrong. No one is forcing the term queer on him. It's simply there for him to use if he feels comfortable doing so. Which he clearly doesn't.

Where he's right is that *queer* is one of a number of what might be called *umbrella terms* to talk about identity—a big, sprawling tent that includes a range of disparate identities that are at once very different from one another but at the same time share a common element. (In this case, a departure from what used to be seen as normative sexual identity and behavior.)

Where Sedaris is again wrong is that the newer terms, more often than not, are not meant to replace the older terms but to complement and supplement them. People can still identify as gay or trans or bisexual. And, if they choose, they can also identify as queer. Similarly, Latinx isn't meant to replace Hispanic or Mexican or South American.

Perhaps the most revealing phrase in Sedaris's commentary is this: "I need a resting place." I understand. The constantly evolving language around identity can be tough to keep up with. But evolve it will, as we individually and collectively will continue to do. There is no resting place. And we should be okay with that.

17

HEADWINDS AND TAILWINDS

As we've discussed, the language with which we typically talk about things like prejudice, privilege, and exclusion tends to be charged. It is charged with vastly different meanings and associations on both sides of our increasingly divided political spectrum. Contested terms or labels quickly become symbols and political footballs in the so-called culture wars. Look at how critical race theory (CRT)—a previously obscure academic field that has been around for decades—has come to serve as a catch-all symbol for a whole range of issues around race and American history that have very little relation to CRT as it is actually taught and studied.

For some, this language is also charged with . . . well, the feeling they are being charged with an offense they don't feel they are guilty of or have very little to do with. The language around race and racism ignites volatile feelings of accusation, guilt, blame, and defensiveness. Later, I will address how these feelings—particularly when mixed with our apprehension about saying the wrong thing—can prevent us from standing up as inclusive leaders. I will discuss how to manage those feelings, how to make peace with the fact that you will indeed mess up and cause harm, and how to repair when you do so.

But for all their imperfections and the conflict they stir up, we need these terms. Although many ideas have been discussed and defined in the previous chapter, there are two concepts that are integral to this work and that I believe warrant their own focused discussion.

Again, I must give credit to Dolly Chugh's book *The Person You Mean to Be: How Good People Fight Bias* for introducing me to talking about privilege—and the lack thereof—in terms of headwinds and tailwinds.* The appeal of these concepts (aside from their political neutrality) is that we can all relate to them immediately and in a very intuitive and visceral way.

Whether it's hiking, running, biking, air travel, or sailing, we have all felt what it's like to have the wind at our backs, almost lifting us and carrying us along. If the tailwind is strong enough and we have caught it just right, we might experience a feeling of effortlessness. If you've ever watched a hawk riding a thermal and flying without having to flap its wings, that is the feeling of ease we might sometimes have with a tailwind at our backs. Conversely, making progress against a headwind can make us feel like we are moving in mud, in slow motion. Every step is an effort, a slog. We feel like we are carrying an invisible weight.

Those contrasting sensations are, in a nutshell, what it's like to move in a system that is geared either to our advantage or our disadvantage. They are a universal experience in many different aspects of life—we have all experienced both, making this common ground we can use to better empathize with one another. Thus, headwinds and tailwinds become a simple metaphor for privilege.

These terms do not discount individual effort or responsibility. Just because you have a tailwind at your back doesn't mean you aren't working

---

* Chugh, *The Person You Mean to Be.*

hard. It doesn't mean you didn't earn the fruits of your labor. But your privilege *is* unearned. Both things can be true.

Someone facing a headwind is still responsible for their own choices and actions. They have to make the best of a given situation. They just have to labor harder for each increment of progress.

———

We could spend chapter upon chapter, a whole book even, unpacking how various groups and identities face different kinds of headwinds and how others benefit from tailwinds. We could look at how these advantages and disadvantages are embedded in culture and systems. In previous examples, I have leaned quite heavily on race and to a lesser extent gender. These identities are often more obvious than others and are forefront in discussions around diversity and inclusion. Others are less so.

We are, it seems, still in the early stages of fully appreciating the full range of expressions of gender identity and sexual orientation. In surveys on psychological safety, LGBTQIA+ folks consistently report high levels of microaggressions.

As Alice Wong points out in the collection she edited, *Disability Visibility*, as many as one in five people in the US lives with a disability.[*] And yet ableism can be a kind of stealth prejudice, in that some disabilities are visible while others are less apparent; all are underrepresented in media and popular culture and shrouded in misunderstanding. (Mental illness is one such largely invisible disability; see sidebar on mental health.)

Neurodivergence is another world of diversity we are just getting a grasp on; here, too, we see that not all difference is physically noticeable.

---

[*] Alice Wong, ed., *Disability Visibility* (New York: Crown Books, 2020).

Current events repeatedly stir up lingering prejudice against Muslims, Asians, and others. I invite you to make a lifelong habit of seeking to learn about the histories, struggles, and triumphs of others.

Mental Health

Mental health is not itself always part of the language of inclusion but is relevant here for a few reasons. The well-known stigma around mental illness—feelings of shame and the concern that bringing the issue up, in the workplace especially, is a sign of weakness—spills over into the broader issue of mental health. We can struggle with our mental health at times without having a diagnosable mental health condition.

There is a reciprocal relationship between mental health and inclusiveness. Leaders need to be able to view mental health through a DEI lens, and conversely, view DEI through a mental health lens. Historically excluded groups likely face different and often more acute mental health challenges and may also deal with stigmas around these issues within their own communities. (That is certainly the case in the Southeast Asian community.)

During the COVID-19 pandemic, symptoms of anxiety and depression ran very high in the Black and Latino communities in particular—both in response to the higher risk and death toll from Covid and the social unrest around the murder of George Floyd. People of color were bringing the burden of these issues with them into the workplace, where they were already more likely to face microaggressions and other slights. Part of the role of the inclusive leader is being attuned to this complex interplay between inclusion and mental health.

Attending to our mental health is an essential part of the well-being of all people. But for those with a diagnosed mental health condition, the workplace can be a tricky place to navigate. Surveys show that a high percentage of employees dealing with mental illness do not get the treatment they need, and inadequate coverage is only part of the problem. Those from marginalized communities may not know where to find help that speaks to their experience, or they may not feel comfortable asking for the time off they need to investigate best-care options.

Many other differences and identities I won't even touch on in this book carry their own headwinds and tailwinds. This Wheel of Privilege graphic suggests the breadth of the landscape of identity and how it plays out in society.

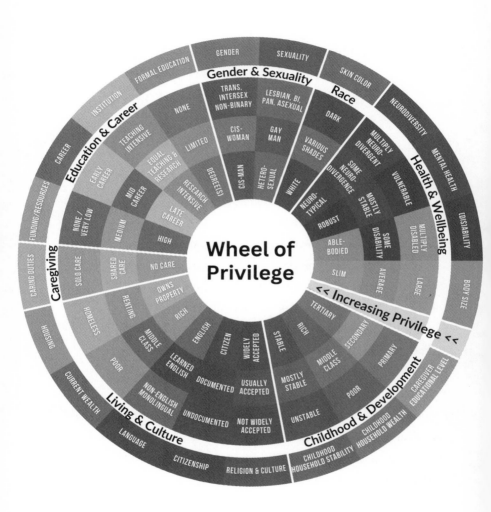

18

A CULTURALLY SENSITIVE LENS

B ias is so baked into the systems that shape our lives (including institutions *and* systems of belief) that it feels almost a given part of
the environment. It is invisible. Which is why I like using the idea of
headwinds and tailwinds to talk about privilege; we notice them because
they're *not* a constant. Sometimes we have the wind at our backs, sometimes we're going into it, sometimes it's calm and there is no wind at all.

But what if we had one or the other and it was always there? It would
be like gravity, a powerful force we have acclimated to so fully we don't
notice or think about it. That unseen quality helps give privilege and bias
their power. The same holds true for any idea (or set of ideas) or assumption baked into our shared culture.

It is largely through the lens of culture that I wish to approach the
work of inclusiveness in the workplace. My professor Marcelo Suárez-
Orozco used to describe culture as the thing that we swim in. Does a fish
"notice" water? Or is water such a constant, ubiquitous, inseparable part of
its existence that it is just taken for granted as part of the way things are?

Culture is like that. Culture is the ideas, images, associations, assumptions, beliefs, and learned responses that we move through. We have some
degree of autonomy and self-determination in choosing how we respond

to the culture. We can push back against it. In concert with others, we can at times redefine it, or parts of it.

But perhaps we don't have the degree of autonomy or self-determination we would like to think we have. If you were raised in a culture that almost universally saw the world as flat, could you break that mold and see it as a sphere? And if your culture saw it as a sphere but one that was at the fixed center of the universe with the stars and other heavenly bodies rotating around us, could you imagine the more complicated reality we now know to be true?

> **Cultural Humility**
>
> Cultural humility is the ability to maintain an interpersonal stance that is other-oriented in relation to aspects of cultural identity that are most important to the other person.
>
> It is a dynamic and lifelong process focusing on self-reflection, personal critique, and acknowledging one's own biases. It recognizes the shifting nature of intersecting identities and encourages ongoing curiosity rather than an endpoint. Cultural humility involves understanding the complexity of identities—that even in sameness there is difference. Leaders must accept they will never be fully aware of the evolving and dynamic nature of another person's experiences.

In the West especially, where there is such a premium placed on individuality and the sanctity and self-determination of the individual, talking about culture can feel a little scary. We prefer to talk about psychology, which operates (or so we like to believe) at the unit of the individual. The link between the two was another formative part of Marcelo's teachings for me: an appreciation for the differences between culture and psychology, and for the intersections and interactions between the two. Exploring that fraught connection is the very ambitious project of Marcelo's field of psychological anthropology.

> **Psychological Anthropology**
>
> Psychological anthropology is the study of psychological topics, like cognition, personality, and emotion, using anthropological concepts and methods, like culture, social experience, and grounded theory. The field is concerned with topics such as narrative, memory, belief, collective trauma, and psychological development as they occur within and across cultures. It also examines the intrapersonal and interpersonal dynamics of how certain cultural phenomena like behaviors and languages play out. Ultimately, psychological anthropology is sensitive to the cultural context in which mental processes occur.

19

NOTABLE EXPERIENCES IN AMERICA

While the scope of this book can't delve into each specific kind of difference, and the particular struggles around privilege, exclusion, and bias that come with those differences, I am going to briefly touch on two experiences that are most prominent in teaching about inclusive leadership.

THE BLACK EXPERIENCE IN AMERICA

It is simply impossible not to give the Black experience in America a special place in our discussion. The 1619 Project of the *New York Times* explored (and not without controversy) not only how slavery and the long aftermath of its abolishment contradict and undermine America's core principles, but how slavery has been a part of American history for over four hundred years.* In the year 1619, the introduction to the Project tells us, a ship carrying twenty slaves arrived at a port in the colony of

---

* "The 1619 Project," *New York Times Magazine* (online), accessed June 24, 2023, https://www.nytimes.com/interactive/2019/08/14/magazine/11619-amer-ica-slavery.html.

Virginia. "No aspect of the history of the country that would be formed has been untouched by the years of slavery that followed." Slavery is not a footnote, an exception, or an oversight; it's an ugly truth that belongs "at the very center of our national narrative."*

It belongs at the center of the narrative around equity and opportunity in the workplace as well. The workplace, and our economy more generally, exhibits all kinds of divides, gaps, and inequities—with race being among the most pervasive and persistent, particularly between Black and white in America.

It also must be pointed out that the protests that erupted in the wake of the murder of George Floyd, and the broader national "racial reckoning" those protests helped trigger, are a big part of why this book exists. We had seen protests in response to the killing of unarmed Black men by police before. But the upheaval that followed this latest outrage galvanized a movement more diverse and sustained than any we've witnessed in quite some time.

I would still be in this line of work had it not been for the murder of George Floyd and the movement it created. But my work would not be getting the same response or reach. In the months after his death, and as it became clear that the police officer responsible would be tried and then convicted, CEOs and companies across the country declared their commitment to fighting against racism and for a more equitable and inclusive workplace. In some cases, these bold statements rang hollow, and companies whose track record wasn't consistent with their high-minded words

---

* Growing up in Canada, it took me a while to fully appreciate this fact.

were quickly called to task for it.

For my part, I have been struck by both a deep desire on the part of corporate leadership to be part of a real change and a deep curiosity as to how to go about doing that. George Floyd's murder and the subsequent ways the 2020 pandemic revealed glaring racial disparities in every facet of American life have been game changers in the discussion of conscious leadership in the workplace.

WOMEN OF COLOR: IDENTITY IS MULTIPLE

The experience of women of color also deserves special mention. When you begin with the historic disadvantages and headwinds for the female gender and stack race on top, those challenges seem to multiply rather than simply add up. We have already seen how representation for women of color drops precipitously at every rung of the corporate ladder—far more so than for women in general. This is one example of *intersectionality*, a term coined by Kimberlé Crenshaw to refer to the framework for understanding how an individual's various social and cultural identities combine to create different degrees of discrimination, privilege, advantage, and disadvantage.

The discussion of women of color also illustrates the broader issue of multiple identities. We are all more than one thing; none of us can or should be reduced to a single defining identity. But the challenge of juggling multiple identities is particularly acute when someone belongs to two (or more) historically marginalized groups. I briefly shared my own childhood experience of being not just a brown girl in a mostly white community but also a minority within the minority South Indian community. The presence of multiple identities creates situations in which belonging and inclusion aren't always what they appear to be.

Deepa Purushothaman, the author of *The First, the Few, the Only: How Women of Color Can Redefine Power in Corporate America*, implores women of color to push back against toxic messaging—externally and internally—about achievement, speaking out, using our voices, "leaning in," or having a seat the table.* We are experiencing an inflection point for women of color; as leaders, we must ask ourselves if we are going to decide to be on the right side of it.

---

* Deepa Purushothaman, *The First, the Few, the Only: How Women of Color Can Redefine Power in Corporate America* (HarperCollins, 2022).

20

THE PROBLEM WITH
THE MODEL MINORITY MYTH

In telling my own story in part I, I touched on the model minority play-book, which is both a narrative and a set of expectations for how certain groups navigate their way through North American society. It is a set of dynamics that has very much informed my own life. The term itself, and the baggage around it, generates a lot of mixed feelings.

The idea began as a kind of compliment, one focused initially on Japanese Americans. In 1966 sociologist William Pettersen wrote a cover story for the *New York Times Magazine* titled "Success Story, Japanese American Style."* The article noted that, despite a history of discrimination and injustice (in particular, large-scale internment camps during World War II, just two decades earlier), Japanese Americans had achieved a great deal of success. Pettersen didn't stop there. He explained their success by focusing on the commitment within Japanese American culture to education and their hard work ethic, family values, and respect for authority. Their success, he summarized, came "by their almost totally unaided effort."

---

* William Pettersen, "Success Story, Japanese American Style," *New York Times Magazine* (January 9, 1966).

Pettersen contrasts the Japanese American "exception" with the norm for what he calls "problem minorities"—in particular, Black Americans. Pettersen's juxtaposition is even more problematic in context: just a year before, Daniel Patrick Moynihan, then President Johnson's assistant secretary of labor, authored a report on the state of Black America that focused largely on the instability of inner-city Black families.* In other words, he noted the absence of the same positive traits Pettersen had praised Japanese Americans for.

In both cases, politics and institutional racism are left out of the equation. The model minority myth (which now includes most but not all Asian Americans) implies that Asian Americans are somehow immune from the challenges faced by other people of color. It ignores an ongoing history of harassment that the stereotypes of the myth actually help perpetuate. The harm of these stereotypes, and the lingering bias and resentment behind them, may not get a lot of press or be obvious to most Americans. But as we saw during the wave of harassment and hate crimes directed at Asian Americans after the outbreak of COVID-19, that historical animus remains just beneath the surface, waiting to be triggered.†

The broad success story for many Asian Americans (which has some truth to it) also obscures high rates of poverty for some communities. While it is true that Asian Americans are well-represented in the student bodies of prominent universities, that has not translated into high rates of representation at the top of most fields, even in high tech.

---

* Daniel Patrick Moynihan, *The Negro Family: The Case for National Action*, Office of Policy Planning and Research, United States Department of Labor, March 1965.

† Similarly, the 9/11 attacks triggered latent Islamophobia. There were also numerous attacks on Sikhs, who are obviously not Muslim, simply because they, too, wear turbans.

The other dark side of the myth is the outsized expectations and pressure it generates—and the resulting shame when expectations haven't been met or there's been a departure from the traditional playbook. Mental health is very much the elephant in the room for many Asian Americans.

The myth certainly cuts both ways, and I can attest from my own experience that it is a source of hugely ambivalent feelings. On the one hand, there is enormous pride in following the success of those of Indian heritage. A much-noted example of the myth is the way Indian American students have dominated the Scripps Spelling Bee. At one point, South Asians had won the annual competition twenty-two times in twenty-three years. I beam with pride for their success. But to the extent that it feeds into stereotypes of the "Asian nerd," that success is also a burden. So I was both relieved and happy when in 2021 Zaila Avant-garde broke that streak and became the first Black US champion. While the myth has evolved since Pettersen's 1966 article, it remains deeply entrenched as the foundation for many harmful stereotypes against Asian Americans. Understanding the roots of stereotypes can help us to dismantle them and manage them, with the hope of accepting people for who they really are.

2 1

A WORD ON STEREOTYPES AND LEARNING

Staying on the topic, I want to share a few thoughts on how stereotypes originate and on how we can collectively move away from them. Not to defend them, but in a way, stereotypes serve a purpose, at least at first.* You might think of them as a rough first sketch of a culture or tradition we find new and unfamiliar. Like a cartoonist's sketch, stereotypes take the qualities we find most unfamiliar and exaggerate them.

Stereotypes can be our initial introduction to a people who might have previously gone unnoticed. In other words, they can be a first (and very imperfect!) step toward visibility and representation.

Let me use an example that intersects with my own heritage: Apu, the Indian convenience store owner from the television series *The Simpsons*. When the show first premiered in 1989, there was virtually no representation for South Asians on either the big screen or the small screen. In terms of pop culture, we were almost invisible. Mindy Kaling and Dev Patel were decades away.

So Apu was a breakthrough. And (unlike, say, Homer Simpson) he was industrious and hard-working. He was, in his own way, a model minority.

---

* But they do indeed often lead to unconscious bias, which I will address later.

But the character—particularly that he was voiced by white actor Hank Azaria—has come under fire.

The topic is the focus of *The Problem with Apu*, a short documentary by comedian Hari Kondabolu.* Kondabolu says there is a condescension, a kind of soft racism, to the broad strokes of the character. As a *New Yorker* article about the film points out, American culture is littered with examples of what one might call positive stereotypes: characters (like Uncle Tom or Charlie Chan) "who were invented to thwart stereotypes only to end up advancing different, softer, no less racist stereotypes in their stead."†

One problem is that, while Apu might once have been a breakthrough, he has never evolved as a character. Kondabolu describes him as a kind of "fossil" trapped in amber. Perhaps there was a missed opportunity to deepen the character and to challenge or break free of the initial stereotype.

A central issue is Azaria's exaggerated Indian accent. Kondabolu interviews a number of other Indian actors and comics who all have had experiences of being bullied or teased—and in which Apu's name or some of his catch phrases were invoked. Kondabolu himself has been heckled during his show by someone calling out, "Thank you, come again."

Azaria declined to appear in the documentary. But in a subsequent interview, he acknowledged the unintended hurt his Indian caricature may have caused and also expressed his hope that both he and the show might learn and evolve going forward. An episode of *The Simpsons* obliquely addressed the controversy (although not in a way that pleased everyone).

In this, I see the beginnings of a learning process—admittedly an

---

* *The Problem with Apu*, written by and starring Hari Kondabolu, directed by Michael Melamedoff (truTV, 2017).
† Hua Hsu, "The Soft Racism of Apu from *The Simpsons*," *New Yorker*, November 16, 2017.

incomplete one. Perhaps a better example of learning playing out publicly in a productive way was a lesser controversy over the singer Lizzo's use of the word *spaz* in her song "Grrrls." In some communities, and in Black slang, the word (used as a verb) connotes going wild and having a good time. But, being short for *spastic*, it also has a long history as a derogatory term describing people with certain disabilities. (Think of how as a kid you might have used the word *retarded* as a casual and harmless insult, though you now know better.)

A fan wrote to Lizzo and pointed this out. Her response was immediate and gracious. She admitted she wasn't aware of the use of the word as an insult and, not wanting to perpetuate any harm, altered the lyric. When some on social media continued to criticize Lizzo, Trevor Noah of *The Daily Show* responded with a spot-on monologue. He pushed back at those who might want to pile on Lizzo for essentially trying and being accountable. And for not having perfect knowledge of every connotation of every word in the first place.*

What Noah did is what I try to do as a matter of operating principle in my work: allow people the grace, and the space, to make mistakes (whatever their intentions); acknowledge and be accountable for any harm; and then attempt to repair and reduce that harm by making a change and examining what biases caused the infraction to happen in the first place. This is how learning happens. Learning doesn't happen when we get everything right the first time. It happens when we stumble.

Even the people (in my view) overreacting to Lizzo's faux pas are going through their own learning process. When I see dustups like these two examples, I don't look for a side to take. I think, *This is what learning looks*

---

* Trevor Noah, "Lizzo's 'Grrrls' Lyric Controversy: Between the Scenes," *The Daily Show*, July 28, 2022, https://www.youtube.com/watch?v=ejBRBZWnotQ.

like. Live, and in real time. With stumbles, missteps, overreactions, and all of the messy stuff that makes us human.

Which isn't to say there aren't times to call people out. But we also need to give people the grace to be human, to learn, to evolve.

22

THE GLUE OF PSYCHOLOGICAL SAFETY

One reason some companies now designate an officer of diversity, equity, inclusion, and *belonging* is that the latter adds a crucial extra bit to the work of inclusion. Or perhaps it simply makes explicit and underscores an element that should already be implied by the first three terms. It is one thing to be included in the room, another to feel you have a seat—an *equal* seat—at the table. But *belonging* goes a little further, a little deeper. It is about being fully welcomed. About being valued, not just for what you do, but for who you are.

This sense of belonging, animated by a critical bond of trust, has come to be known as *psychological safety*. This is the freedom to be your authentic self at work, the feeling that your voice is respected and valued, and the permission to take risks.

Research into this critical dynamic began, in more than one sense, with mistakes.

ORGANIZATIONAL BEHAVIOR: A HOSPITAL CASE STUDY

As I suspect is already clear to you, the road to inclusive leadership is very much an imperfect one. It is full of potholes and speed bumps that we will step into or collide with. At times it will feel as though we have veered onto the shoulder or off the road altogether. We have to accept this as the ebb and flow of the learning process. We have to give ourselves (and others) the grace to make mistakes, to learn from them, and to get better.

In the 1990s, Amy Edmondson was a PhD student at Harvard studying organizational behavior.* She began visiting and studying hospital wards in the Boston area. Her hypothesis was that good teamwork and good medicine would go hand in hand. She developed a set of criteria by which she could assess the strength and cohesiveness of various teams. She looked at which teams were characterized by informal conversation among staff, team leaders who set clear goals, and an environment where conflicts were addressed openly. She measured individual satisfaction, happiness, and self-motivation.

She assumed that the units with the strongest sense of teamwork would have the lowest error rates. But in fact, the data told the opposite story. Was she herself making a mistake?

She checked the data again. Then she looked more closely at the responses of individual nurses to certain questions. One question and set of responses jumped out at her: "If you make a mistake in this unit, will it be held against you?"

Edmondson had her aha moment. It wasn't that staff on the strongest teams were making more errors. It was that they were comfortable reporting them.

There was an additional wrinkle as well. On some strong teams that

---

* Amy Edmondson, "Psychological Safety and Learning Behavior in Work Teams," *Administrative Science Quarterly* 44, no. 2 (1999): 350–383. https://doi.org/10.2307/2666999.

scored well on Edmondson's initial measures of cohesion, nurses still didn't feel comfortable admitting mistakes. It wasn't cohesion within a team that mattered; it was the informal culture—a culture characterized by what she would come to call psychological safety.

Crucially, it wasn't just about the informal culture among team members. It was also about leadership. One nurse sums up how both of these elements come together, "There is an unspoken rule here to help each other and check each other. People feel more willing to admit to errors here, because the nurse manager goes to bat for you."

PROJECT ARISTOTLE

Google also eventually arrived at the conclusion that psychological safety was the secret sauce for great teams—but by an entirely different route. In 2012, the company's Peoples Analytics division set out to pinpoint why some teams performed better than others. The effort was code-named Project Aristotle (a nod to Aristotle's quote about the whole being greater than the sum of its parts).

Google has a highly individualistic culture. So they initially focused on group composition: What composition of individuals with different skills, backgrounds, and temperaments made for the best teams? Google loves data, and they excel at identifying patterns. But no matter how many different ways they combed the data on team composition, there were no underlying patterns. As one manager put it, the "who" didn't seem to matter.

So they turned to the "how"—to the group norms and unspoken rules that make for team culture. And once they focused on group norms and team culture, they came to the same conclusions as Amy Edmondson and actually drew on her research. It was psychological safety that set the best teams apart. As Edmondson summed up in her 1999 study: psychological safety is found in "a team climate characterized by interpersonal trust and mutual respect in which people are comfortable being themselves" and "a shared belief that the team is safe for interpersonal risk-taking."*

As Google looked at data from metrics that weren't their original focus, they found a significant element of team culture: equality in conversation turn-taking. "As long as everyone got a chance to talk, the team did well," one of the researchers said. "But if only one person or a small group spoke all the time, the collective intelligence declined."

INCLUSIVITY LEADS TO PSYCHOLOGICAL SAFETY

Recent research has only confirmed these conclusions. Psychological safety—which requires individuals, both team members and leaders, with strong interpersonal skills, such as emotional intelligence, and an organizational culture of trust and respect—is the key to high-performing teams. It is a major factor in employee satisfaction and well-being and in the ability of companies to attract and retain talent.

The role of psychological safety in inclusive leadership should be fairly obvious, but I'll spell it out. Taking the chance to offer new ideas or try out new innovations that might not work out clearly requires a degree of professional risk. The nurses whom Amy Edmondson studied certainly took a great deal of risk in admitting errors in a setting where mistakes can have life or death consequences.

Yet there is a different (and in a sense more acute and intimate) risk in talking frankly and openly about privilege, bias, and exclusion, and about the subtleties in which racism, sexism, and homophobia play out. It takes

---

* Edmondson, "Psychological Safety."

great courage to drop your defenses and enter such conversations with total vulnerability. I see that courage in many JEDI© workshops I lead.

Think, for example, of the white man who acknowledges a growing awareness of biases he didn't even know he had. Or the Asian woman articulating to her colleagues her pent-up frustration about years of slights and microaggressions, and about holding back her feelings because she didn't want to appear weak or oversensitive.

These vulnerable moments are essential to building an inclusive organizational culture, and they don't happen without a firm foundation of psychological safety. Psychological safety isn't easy to build, and it doesn't happen overnight.

The good news? The process of cultivating psychological safety will pay off in spades, in more ways than you can imagine. All of the leadership muscles you and your team members develop in pursuit of an inclusive culture will make you better leaders in general.

If there are just a handful of big takeaways I wish you to draw from this book, one of them is this: the most inclusive leaders are the best leaders, period.

To put it another way: you will never achieve psychological safety in your organization without building an inclusive culture. There is no more rigorous method for cultivating psychological safety than the pursuit of inclusiveness.

⸻

I'm not a hardcore *Star Wars* fan. So when I came up with the JEDI© acronym, it was a happy accident that it coincided with these intergalactic champions for justice. I didn't give the connection much thought beyond that.

Later I read a classic quote from one of the movies in which Obi-Wan Kenobi (played by the great actor Alec Guinness) tells the young Luke Skywalker about the Force. "The Force is what gives a Jedi his power. It's an energy field created by all living things. It surrounds us and penetrates us. It binds the galaxy together."*

Not a bad description, really, for what psychological safety and a deep sense of belonging, trust, and inclusiveness can do for your organization.

---

* *Star Wars: Episode IV - A New Hope*, written and directed by George Lucas, produced by Gary Kurtz, 1977; Twentieth Century Fox, Lucasfilm.

PART III

THE PRACTICE
OF INCLUSIVE
LEADERSHIP

23

DEEP DEMOCRACY

et's get this out in the open from the start: embarking on the work of inclusive leadership can be scary. Time and time again, I see leaders coming to DEI work with great commitment but also an underlying sense of trepidation. They are worried about saying or doing the wrong thing. More than anything else, they are afraid of offending someone, of hurting someone's feelings. So they tighten up and employ a variety of defensive measures, including deflection. They play it safe. They avoid taking risks.*

Playing it safe will not get you where you want to be. The only way to build a truly inclusive culture (and the only way to build a thriving organizational culture, period) is by being fearless, authentic, and vulnerable. Letting your defenses down is never easy. And it's especially difficult in building inclusive leadership, where you may well feel there are potential land mines all around you. Guess what? You're probably going to step in one of those eventually. But you've got to take the leap anyway, knowing

---

* As you've seen, I've had my moments of doubt and trepidation as well. I used to hesitate more before speaking up. Such as at LightHouse, when my first instinct was just to keep my head down and "do my time." But I got used to the discomfort and found out that I could usually recover from my mistakes. I found out, as well, that this was the best way to learn.

that you can attempt to repair and trusting that we can forgive or accept the sometimes hard consequences of learning.

Remember, most everyone on your team is feeling some variation of anxiety or trepidation. The middle-aged white guy doesn't feel qualified to speak about racism. The young Black woman doesn't want to sabotage her career by being seen as "the angry Black woman" or as constantly "playing the race card." After reaching an initial agreement on the broad objective of creating a safe and welcoming environment, a lot of people will want to hold back and play it safe, all for their own diverse reasons.

You as a leader have to make it safe for them to *not* play it safe. The best way you can do that is by modeling fearlessness, authenticity, and vulnerability.

I say all of this at the outset to clear the air and to disabuse you of the notion that your inclusive journey as an individual or as an organization is going to be all unity and harmony. There are going to be bumps in the road, what appear to be setbacks, and some seriously difficult and uncomfortable conversations. Those challenging moments are not obstacles in your inclusive journey. That is leadership.

———

A number of years ago, I encountered and later studied the Lewis Method of Deep Democracy; it profoundly informs my approach to coaching in general, and especially to DEI work. Myrna and Greg Lewis experimented with a new approach to conflict that built on the work of Arnold Mindell when they were hired in the 1990s to help a large South African company work through the legacy of apartheid. The violently oppressive apartheid regime that ruled South Africa for almost fifty years was one of the most brutal in history. In its wake, the country had an enormous divide of anger, fear, and distrust between whites and Blacks. The process of reconciliation has not been easy, at the national level or at the level of individual communities, companies, or organizations.

So why was the Lewis Method so successful in such a divided and potentially volatile situation? At the heart of Deep Democracy is the mindset that—in the right context, with the right leadership—tension is a good thing. The Lewis Method calls for leaning into tension, and leaning into it hard, rather than shying away from it or trying to smooth it over or tamp it down.

It's not just tension for the sake of tension. The tension rising to the surface is a manifestation of a deeper tension below. Again, it is essential that leadership set the right tone and that the group has healthy norms in place—healthy, *inclusive* norms. Above all, it has to be clear that all voices will be heard, valued, and considered. In fact, an inclusive environment in which all voices are expressed virtually guarantees there will be tension and conflict, which is one reason why disagreement is seen as a healthy sign.

Another core concept of the Lewis Method is that there is *wisdom in dissent*. When someone resists the majority, the status quo, or a statement by leadership or a peer, that resistance isn't coming out of the blue. Something is being said or done to provoke that resistance.

So the resistance, the friction, is a healthy sign that you are onto something. The appropriate next step is not to try to resolve the tension but to dig deeper into it—to, as I like to put it, go below the waterline.* If as a group you dig deeply and fearlessly enough, you will find gold.

Deep Democracy also encourages us to keep leaning into discomfort and resistance even after a decision has been made. (As opposed to the

---

* A phrase I likely first encountered in Arnold Mindell's book *The Leader as Martial Artist*, in which he also first sets out his ideas about Deep Democracy.

standard approach of just trying to get everyone to "move on.") Dissenters are asked what they would need in order to be able to come along with the majority decision. This is an act of radical inclusion. This process continues to find the wisdom in dissent and does the hard work of forging unity within disagreement.

All too often, however, companies and organizations don't take the time to do all that digging and properly air things out. As a result, unresolved tension, contradiction, or conflict stays below the waterline—where, unnamed and unaddressed, it will silently but surely undermine the culture.

24

UNITY MUST BE EARNED

Unity is sometimes invoked as a reason for tamping down conflict rather than fully exploring it, as if unity were simply the absence of tension. When I see this dynamic play out, I think of Dr. Martin Luther King's distinction between a positive peace, which is the presence of justice, and a negative peace, which is the absence of tension. A negative peace dressed up as unity is not a meaningful unity. Unity can't simply be invoked; it must be earned.

I also think of my former teacher Marcelo, who would point out that each individual will experience unity differently. This is especially the case when there are deeply contested issues at stake. The Lewis Method begins with an earnest attempt to see the issue from all points of view. Yet in an organization, decisions must be made, and at some point, the group will take a vote and everyone must take a side. If the process of hearing and considering every viewpoint is meaningful and the decision-making process is transparent, people will buy into and respect the ultimate decision.

That doesn't mean they have to feel good about it. Unity is sometimes confused with harmony, with feeling good. Deep Democracy, while it may keep the group together and prevent it from falling apart, doesn't necessarily bring about harmony. In fact, just as an initial tension is often a good sign, lingering discomfort even after a decision has been reached shows that difference, diversity, and disagreement are alive and well.

So, no: Unity is not harmony, nor is it consensus. It is often messy.

A FLEETING MOMENT OF UNITY

A telling example of how a simplistic notion of unity can actually tear an organization apart can be found in the response of the media group Axios to two different upheavals in American political life. As protests following the murder of George Floyd started breaking out across the country, the leadership of Axios went out of their way to give employees the green light to participate if they were moved to do so: "We proudly support and encourage you to exercise your rights to free speech, press, and protest," the company's chief executive wrote. "If you're arrested or meet harm while exercising these rights, Axios will stand behind you and use the Family Fund to cover your bail or assist with medical bills."[*]

Two years later, when the Supreme Court overturned *Roe v. Wade*, the company took a very different tack and urged employees to stay on the sidelines. "Abortion is a human-rights issue that has become a highly politicized topic, with very specific policies being debated in Washington and in most states," the CEO wrote. "So it seems impossible to march—or tweet opinions—and not be perceived as picking a political side in public . . . [and] could undermine our trusted journalism."[†]

---

[*] Edmond Lee and Ben Smith, "Axios Allows Its Reporters to Join Protests," *New York Times* (June 8, 2020). https://www.nytimes.com/2020/06/08/business/media/axios-allows-reporters-protest-march.html.
[†] Laura Wagner, "Axios to Staff: Our Values Are Cynically Engineered and Incoherent," *Defector* (May 11, 2022). https://defector.com/axios-to-staff-our-values-are-cynically-engineered-and-incoherent.

When employees called the CEO out over how inconsistent this was with his encouraging people to participate in the George Floyd protests, he explained that his previous statement was issued "before specific policy solutions were being debated. It was a fleeting moment of unity."

In other words, unity in this case is people marching arm-in-arm. And, as long as there is harmony, then openly voicing opinions is okay. But as soon as things get difficult or politicized, or specific policies are on the table—then debate and the public airing of opinions is divisive and should be discouraged.

I don't mean to make light of the dilemma Axios faced. Navigating the process of how divisive social issues play out in an organization isn't easy, and a media company does have an interest in having its employees appear fair and unbiased. But this is the opposite of the Deep Democracy approach. And, far from avoiding conflict, his attempt to tamp down debate and opinion proved deeply divisive.

2 5

EMOTIONAL INTELLIGENCE: THE WHAT

Democracy and debate are messy, whether in society at large, within an organization, or in a small team meeting. Which is why it is so important to be able to read people, to gauge their emotional and mental state, and then to respond accordingly. This is especially important when you are tackling inclusiveness and volatile issues like racism, sexism, and privilege. You have to learn to notice people's anxieties, hesitations, and fears, and address them. Only then will you be able to create those big, powerful spaces where people can thrive and be accepted, and where you and your team can fearlessly explore the questions that will help you create a more inclusive culture.

If it sounds like we're talking about psychological safety, which is where we ended part II, you're exactly right. But before we talk about establishing that all-important atmosphere in your organization, we must first discuss the practice of reading people, the room, and yourself, and incorporating that information in how you lead. This practice is now widely recognized as an essential business skill set and has come to be known as emotional intelligence, or EI. It is also sometimes represented as EQ, a direct nod to IQ or intelligence quotient—a parallel that shows being intelligent with our emotions is just as important as being intelligent with our intellect. Moreover, although we sometimes fall into the trap of interpreting emotion and reason as opposites and in conflict with one another, researchers have established that, in fact, they work hand in hand in surprising ways.

Reading others is important, yes. But in many ways, emotional intelligence starts with being able to read yourself. Our own emotions can guide us and offer essential insight and clarity—but only if we are cognizant of them. Emotional intelligence at this basic level is a kind of ongoing mindfulness practice. While we don't want to be self-involved and constantly immersed in our own emotions, a part of our awareness needs to regularly scan our emotional state and look for signs of anxiety or discomfort. When we see those signs, we have to name what's happening and then inquire as to why certain feelings are arising. This posture of open awareness and curiosity can help defuse volatile emotions. Being aware of our own emotional state puts us in a position to manage that state, to exercise emotional self-control, and also to be clear and transparent about how we're feeling.*

These two skill sets (self-awareness and self-management) constitute the first two quadrants of a model of emotional intelligence first developed by the psychologist Daniel Goleman. They naturally and organically spill over into how we interact with others. When we are able to clearly read and understand our own emotions, we can also more clearly recognize their impact on others. This awareness allows us to modify, if needed,

---

* This practice can be difficult for some and easier for others. Some neurodivergent experiences, for example, can make it especially challenging or impossible to recognize emotions in the self and in others. Emotional intelligence is not adequately inclusive of neurodivergence. This is one of many reasons why emotional intelligence is problematic, which we will discuss further in chapter 33, "Emotional Intelligence: Reconsidered."

how we are expressing those emotions.

As we expand out from the self to others, emotional intelligence becomes more about social awareness (the third of Goleman's quadrants). This is about empathy, active listening, and the ability to exercise broad organizational awareness—reading not just individuals but the emotional dynamics of the group as a whole. As with self-awareness, social awareness positions us to better manage our relationships (Goleman's final quadrant is relationship management), to inspire others, to guide them on the path to more fully developing themselves, to manage conflict, to build relationships, to foster teamwork and collaboration.

Developing these very basic (but often difficult) skills of self-awareness and social awareness and then translating those insights into how we act and lead, are cornerstones of inclusive leadership. There's also a great deal of research confirming that these so-called soft skills go a long way toward better leadership, period.

Of course, the expression of emotions is culturally defined. You may have come up against certain expressions, phrases, or behaviors that are appropriate in your own culture, but are inappropriate elsewhere, only learning that they were inappropriate through people's reactions or feedback to you. That kind of learning is an example of building cultural intelligence. Cultural intelligence (CQ) refers to a person's ability to adapt, adjust, and be sensitive as they interact with people from different cultures. And emotional intelligence is bolstered by cultural intelligence. Both are foundational to inclusive leadership.

Beyond the buzzwords and the metrics, I want to talk for a moment about my vision of what makes a great leader. Great leaders are agile, perceptive, self-aware, and curious. They are kind, direct, fallible, brave, and vulnerable. They are diverse, changing, developing, and learning.

My developmental psychology lens is very much in evidence here, I know. Great leaders are constantly evolving and looking to help others evolve. Part of how they stay that way is being mindful of the fact that leadership (as complex and multifaceted as it can seem at times) really comes down to two things: behaviors and mindsets. Which again is why emotional intelligence is so important. When your behavior and your mindset are informed by a high degree of EI, you will more often than not do the right thing.

To be clear: it won't necessarily be the perfect thing. With inclusive leadership especially, we have to get beyond the binary of getting it right or doing it wrong. We should, instead, keep our eyes on the prize—the big prizes—of unity, safety, and humanity. If we attend to those overarching values and concentrate on building and nurturing relationships, we'll get it right enough.

———

Inclusive leadership can be daunting. The term alone, and much of the language around it, can deter some from "taking the leap." Keep it simple, and make it less daunting, by focusing on behavior and mindset. Those are your most powerful tools in addressing adaptive challenges.

Adaptive challenges are harder to identify and may require a more multifaceted approach than technical challenges. They may require changes in roles, values, and beliefs or the capacity to think "outside the box"; they may require multiple changes in multiple places simultaneously, and they may not have an obvious solution.

A technical challenge usually has a straightforward solution that can be quickly implemented, such as designing an ad campaign for your latest product. In this case, the marketing process is well defined and best practices are established. It may not be effortless, but there is a process that can be followed and experts can easily execute on the challenge.

You cannot successfully tackle an adaptive challenge without keeping a clear focus on behavior and mindset, on building relationships, and on the skills of emotional intelligence.

26

EMOTIONAL INTELLIGENCE: THE HOW

SELF-AWARENESS

So, how do you actually go about developing your own EI and fostering those same qualities in others? Let's start with self-awareness. If, broadly, emotional intelligence is the foundation for building psychological safety, then understanding yourself is the foundation for emotional intelligence. You cannot manage your emotional reactions to difficult and challenging conversations if you aren't attuned to your own emotional life. And you won't be able to tune in and respond appropriately to the emotional reactions of others if you can't effectively manage your own emotions.

Understanding yourself is a deeper and more layered process than the popular term *self-awareness* might indicate. First, it very much *is* a process; it is a lifelong journey. Understanding yourself is a constellation of many concepts, including being aware of your needs, values, and beliefs; knowing your preferences, tendencies, and styles; observing your behaviors and actions (and the impact they have on you and others); and how these things are changing over time. Self-awareness requires us to listen deeply to ourselves and to others, to take information about ourselves from multiple sources, and to evaluate that information and incorporate any new insights into our future words and actions.

People are sometimes surprised when I highlight being in touch with your own needs as an essential element of self-awareness. Especially when we are talking about this in the context of learning how to be a more empathetic and inclusive leader who is responsive to the needs of others and not just wrapped up in their own narrative. But you have needs; we all do. And when you know who you are and what you need, you can find ways to fulfill your needs. If you're not mindfully attending to your own needs, that doesn't mean those needs go away. Your unmet needs will leak out in your words and deeds in ways you don't even realize.

This was a hard lesson for me to learn. Growing up with Indian immigrant parents who defined for me what they believed I needed—to do well in school and get a lucrative job, for example—suppressed my ability to recognize that I have needs, let alone define them for myself. I've noticed this same pattern in many underrepresented people; the invitation to ask for what you need is met with resistance and confusion. "I've never been taught to ask for anything, but rather be grateful for what I got." I understand this so deeply. But having needs doesn't mean you're not grateful; it means you're human.

One example of a surface need we all experience is a desire, on some level, to look good, to make a presentable appearance. To meet this need, you may go to the store and try on a new outfit. You know what fits, looks good, and makes you feel your best. You also know immediately what types of clothes you'll leave on the rack and what types of clothes you'd like to try on. You may also judge yourself as you look in the mirror (who doesn't?) or tell yourself you look ugly. Self-awareness allows you to notice these thoughts, which allows you to change the way you talk to and ultimately see yourself—maybe you now give yourself a pep talk or tell yourself you're beautiful.

In a big-picture sense, this is what self-awareness is about: seeing yourself, trying on things, leaving things behind, keeping some things that make you feel good, and understanding who you are. This awareness relates to psychological safety because, when you're in a room with other people, you can discern what kinds of behaviors and conditions make you feel good and beautiful or bad and unwelcome, and you can adjust accordingly. When Sheela, my dance teacher, spoke to me in Kannada, I didn't feel welcome. I felt confused and different; I wished I understood Kannada, too, so that I could *belong* with that group of kids who spoke the same language as her. But when my sister gave me a knowing glance across the room, indicating that she, too, was lost, I felt seen and no longer alone.

Paying attention to yourself and your own needs is important in another sense as well. Self-awareness is a dynamic and fluid process. It is not just about paying attention to who we are now, but also to who we are becoming. Who we are is a moving target. To return to the clothes analogy, we are always trying on new things and experimenting with how we think of ourselves, how we present to others. Our identity is ever evolving. When we pay attention to this process in ourselves, we can be more responsive to that same process in others.

THE THIRD ENTITY

As you can perhaps already see, the skills for self-awareness translate naturally into social and situational awareness: the art of paying attention to the emotional states and reactions of others. Awareness of self and awareness of others are more intimately connected than you might first think. There is something that exists in the space between you and me to which we both contribute, but which has a life of its own. In coaching, we call this the *third entity*. Think of it as somewhat comparable to *culture* within an organization: the values and norms that animate the shared interpersonal space a group occupies. Put in a more folksy way: it is the way we are with one another.

The space between people is complex, rich, and fraught. A lot happens in that space. It can be a place of unity, alignment, and harmony; it can also be a place of misunderstanding, judgement, distraction, and exclusion. If you can understand what's going on in that space and honor it by giving it language, you can bridge the distance and create more experiences of inclusion rather than exclusion. So what does it take to understand that space, that third entity?

Curiosity, first. Our brains are quick to judge and also quick to label something a threat. Yet we can consciously curate curiosity by observing with equanimity, asking open-ended questions, and listening with openness. I can't overstate how important these qualities are in inclusive leadership—and how difficult they are to maintain in charged or challenging circumstances.

Empathy is a close and related quality. My adviser at Harvard, Bob Selman, studied the development of empathy in children, and his teachings are the building blocks of my work on leadership development. Bob thinks of empathy as the ability to take another person's perspective. This effort is more about understanding emotion than thought.

So can you truly step inside someone else's shoes? Not entirely. My personal spin on empathy (in keeping with the broad themes of this book) is that it is the *attempt* to understand another person's perspective. I use the word *attempt* because it maintains the act of inclusion but gives us a bit more grace and permission to get it wrong. Even when someone gets you wrong, most of the time you can appreciate the effort and intention to understand you. Moreover, if they truly want to understand you, getting you wrong gives you a chance to clarify who you are—for your benefit and theirs. By now you are used to me saying this, but I'll say it again: inclusion is not about getting it right; it's about learning, calibrating, and trying again.

Which is why empathy must be paired with curiosity. Just as important as the effort to understand someone is the sincere desire to do so.

27

LISTENING

No activity is more critical to emotional intelligence—specifically to empathy—than the act of listening.* We all know that listening is vitally important. And most of us sense that authentic, deep listening doesn't occur nearly enough. But we rarely break down listening as a complex and layered skill set. We don't take the time to unpack the mechanics of good listening.

If I asked you, "What is good listening?" you would have an intuitive sense of the answer, even if you couldn't put it into words. You know what good listening is because you have experienced it. Someone listened well to you at some point in your life, and you crave more of it. It feels so good, so essential, when someone listens well to you. When you attempt to understand someone, you are showing an interest and curiosity in them. They are able to show you who they are. That last bit is key: listening is not just about understanding their words but about affirming

---

* I want to recognize that "listening" effectively with our ears (our sense of hearing) is the dominant culture's way of talking about the skill of paying attention and taking in another's words, perspective, and energy. This skill is going to be practiced and experienced differently for people who are deaf or hard of hearing, or blind and hard of seeing.

who they are. It is liberating and sets in motion an entire chain reaction in how you interact with others and the world.

This basic exchange is the essence of belonging and a building block of inclusion. Yet if it is so basic, and so essential, why does it seem so rare and elusive, and so special and precious when it does happen?

After years of doing this work and coaching listening as a particular skill, my hunch is that we fear we are giving up something if we completely commit to listening. We think we might have to suspend our own need to be understood, seen, and heard. Listening is indeed a radical act of giving space to someone; yes, it can feel as though we are giving more than we are receiving. If you think of space as limited, you can easily fall into the trap of thinking of the exchange as a zero-sum game: to the extent I generously give space, I have less for myself.

Yet the remarkable thing about deep listening is that it is *not* zero-sum; it is additive and generative. It expands the space of the third entity; you give *and* get space when you really listen, and you emerge from the experience with a deeper sense of belonging yourself. It is (to fall back on a cliché) the gift that keeps on giving.

ME CHANNEL, YOU CHANNEL

Listening is generative only when it is a nuanced and active two-way street between you and the other person. For the sake of simplification, let's break listening down into two channels: the Me channel and the You channel.* In the Me channel, you continue to listen to your inner voice even as you listen to the other person talking. You're hearing an inner

---

* Powers, Lauren. (2023). *How to Listen Out Loud: Ridiculously Powerful Skills for Leading, Relating, and Happifying,* Pluck Publications.

dialogue that might sound something like, *She's told this story before . . .* That inner dialogue can also involve mentally rehearsing how we plan to respond: *He thinks* he's *busy. Wait till I tell him about the week I've had!* Or we might be multitasking and thinking about a nagging detail that has nothing to do with the conversation: *Shoot, I forgot to get rice for dinner tonight.*

In each of these scenarios, we can still be making a sincere effort to listen to the other person even though there are those times when we tune out and our inner dialogue dominates. We shouldn't immediately assume that Me-type listening is bad and selfish. It is our gateway to relating to someone and thus to empathy. For example, if someone is excitedly sharing an accomplishment with you, it is perfectly natural for that to elicit memories of your own accomplishments: *I remember when I was his age and made my first big leap on the career ladder. That was huge for me. I'm so happy for him!* You might even share that experience, without making it all about you. The combination of relating and sharing can deepen your connection.

On a practical level, Me listening is also important when the situation calls on you to listen on your own behalf. For example, when your physician is giving you a diagnosis, you'd better be listening in the Me channel. Or when your manager or a colleague is offering you some feedback, at least part of you will want to be Me listening so that you can relate the information you're hearing to your own experience.

To be sure, Me listening is not always the best way to listen. It can distract you from fully paying attention to the other person. Let's face it, we've all been in conversations where we can tell the other person's mind is elsewhere. It's not a great feeling. Focusing on the Me channel can lead others to feel excluded, dismissed, or ignored—exactly the opposite of what you're going for as an inclusive leader.

Many situations call for us to switch to the You channel: when your attention is fully *over there* and you are making a conscious effort to tamp down your inner dialogue. You're taking in not only the words the other person is saying but also their nonverbals: pace, volume, and tone. You're taking stock of what is *not* being said. You are engaging multiple senses and faculties of attention. And because we can't entirely shut off our inner dialogue, You listening requires a special effort—which is also what makes it generous and inclusive. Your central impulse when listening in the You channel is to listen and respond with empathy and curiosity. In contrast with the earlier example, if a colleague is sharing an accomplishment and you are listening in the You channel, you aren't relating it to your own accomplishments but looking to learn more about their experience: "That's so exciting. What about it was most rewarding to you?" At its best, You listening expresses acceptance of who the other person is and invites them to be more fully themselves.

As the scenario of a colleague sharing an accomplishment makes clear, both Me and You listening have their merits. During JEDI© workshops, we do exercises where we practice what it's like to approach a conversation in one channel or the other, just to get a clear sense of how the two experiences contrast. In practice, it is rare that we are entirely in one channel or the other. Different situations call for a tailored mix of the two. In one situation, it might be natural and appropriate to relate a colleague's present achievement to a past one of our own. In another situation, that could come across as self-centered. It's a judgment call.

We certainly don't want to fall into the trap of thinking the Me channel is selfish and that the You channel is inherently superior. In the scenario of a doctor-patient conversation, we want our doctor to listen to us with compassion. But we don't want them to be entirely in the You channel. We need for them to be listening to their inner voice, comparing the symptoms to previous patients, attending to their bedside manner, or referencing a recent study published in a medical journal.

ENGAGED LISTENING

Sometimes (and often with the best of intentions) we slip into a lazy conception that listening is purely the act of receiving. In this mindset, our objective is to get the other person's words right, to be able to accurately repeat their words. Our aim should not be to be a good court stenographer! The larger goal should be *engagement*—with listening at the center, intertwined and inseparable from the following related skills: preparation, focus, presence, asking questions, specificity, and synthesizing.*

If listening is an invitation to others to open up, it is also an invitation to ourselves to be curious, to explore, to take chances, to be vulnerable, to risk getting it wrong. What if, in stepping far from the safety of the court stenographer model, we synthesize what we have heard with a past conversation to move toward a new, larger understanding and we get what the other person said wrong? That's not a disaster; it's an opportunity for the other person to clarify. Or maybe we don't get it quite right, but in taking a chance, we have articulated a nascent thought that until now they hadn't been able to put into words.

Listening is not just about receiving. It is also about participation. It is about moving toward another person, another understanding. This is the world of exploring, of expanding and enriching the third entity. In this

---

* Beth McMurtrie, "Teaching: Is It Time to Redefine Class Participation?" newsletter, *Chronicle of Higher Education*, September 8, 2022. I owe this list of related and bundled activities to teacher Mark Sample of Davidson College, who was quoted in this newsletter in a conversation about taking a more expansive look at what it means to think of class participation.

more layered conception, listening is made up of multiple micro-decisions about what to pay attention to. The challenge is to navigate the situation and read the room so you can judge what requires your attention at any given moment.

PASSIVE LISTENING

Passive listening—in other words, anything short of the kind of active listening that is part of the larger process of engagement just discussed—sometimes presents itself as a form of deference and respect. And that may very well be the intention, particularly in a dynamic where you are on the side of privilege. But in the end, passive listening is a way to play it safe. The hard work of inclusion, by contrast, demands risk.

We can see a particular form of passive listening when the more privileged person in an asymmetric relationship suspends their critical faculties. If, for example, you are a white person talking with an Asian American, you may tell yourself you have no right to question their take on racism. Humility is good, but you can't let it handcuff you. It is appropriate to acknowledge that a person of color has a lived experience of racism that you don't, to give credence to their experience and to the conclusions they draw from it, and to suspend your own judgment while you take in their perspective.

But no one Asian American person speaks for all Asian American people. (They're not looking for the job, and it shouldn't put it on them!) No social identity group is monolithic; opinions and experiences vary widely within those groups, and individuals in those groups can be fallible, wrong, or partly right. It is your prerogative—and your obligation as an active participant in the work of inclusion—to consider everything critically. Yes, listen with an open and curious heart and mind. But engage the full spectrum of activities related to active listening we discussed earlier. Especially synthesis: How does what you're hearing square with other things you've read and heard? What does your gut tell you? What unresolved questions do you have? This is the power of curiosity, which good listening often yields.

Giving voice to those questions isn't disrespectful. Engaging someone in real dialogue is the ultimate form of respect. That is how you move along the Ally Continuum from being aware—but largely on the sidelines—to being active—but not fully identified with the cause—to engaging in the full partnership of being an advocate.*

Listening and voice are not separate—they are, in fact, intimately connected. Just as, in the human body, any motion requires opposite muscle groups to engage in a complementary process of give and take, so the active work of inclusive leadership involves a dynamic interplay between listening and voice. Listening and becoming attuned to your own inner voice—and all the questions and confusion that come with it—is the first step in that process.

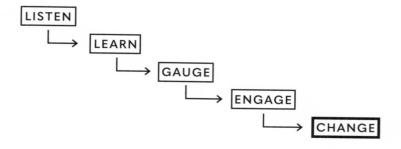

---

* We will more fully discuss the Ally Continuum in chapter 30.

28

VOICE

"What do I have to say about racism? I'm just a middle-aged white guy."

I can't tell you how many times I've heard some variation of that line. I want to acknowledge that there is an element of good intent here, a show of humility, of a willingness to listen first. But the point of what I call the "shut up and listen" admonition from underrepresented people isn't to listen and *stay* shut up (and thus on the sidelines). That's a cop out. The point is to listen *first*. Listening is the beginning, not the end.

Yes, that does sometimes involve biting your tongue and resisting the urge to immediately weigh in on an issue in which those with lived experience in the matter should be heard first. But what comes *after* listening is just as important, and is the real test of allyship.

Exercising your voice involves risk. You might mess up. Most of those mistakes can be redeemed.* But as you start to take the leap and begin using your voice more, keep this in mind as well: Words can wound, but so can silence. Sometimes the harm caused by silence is even harder to repair.

---

* Although, as we will discuss later, some harm is irreparable.

YOUR UNIQUE VOICE

Let's step back and consider what exactly voice is. It is much more than an opinion or perspective. Ultimately it boils down to this simple truth: You are unique and have a unique contribution to offer the world. Your ideas, thoughts, and feelings are yours and yours alone; they help make you *you*. And your voice is an important reflection of that unique self.

Most of us understand in a visceral way that we have a voice, and that using it can be powerful. From a young age we hear phrases like, "Speak up!" (Or the other side of the coin: "Shut up!") So our voice clearly matters. It amplifies who we are. And that amplification puts us out into the world. It is our platform for broadcasting to the world: This is me. See me. Hear me.

That amplification, that act of broadcasting, can be scary. What if I say the wrong thing? What if I misrepresent myself? What if people reduce me to just one thing I've said? Those are valid concerns, ones that we've addressed and will continue to address in the context of inclusive leadership. But we cannot let fear get in the way of being our best and most authentic self. Using your voice is a skill, and like any skill, it takes practice. And reflection and introspection. And (surprise!) experimentation, which by now you know I'm a big fan of.

So let's try to take the scary out of using your voice and consider ways of making this task more manageable—and maybe even enjoyable.

ELEMENTS OF VOICE

Especially when faced with a daunting task, it can be helpful to break it up into small chunks. You can do that with voice, which is in fact comprised of many different elements. Our audible voice has aspects like pace, volume, tone, inflection, and amplification. Singers know these nuances and how and when to accentuate them.

Voice, of course, is not just the audible product of our vocal cords. And, in the spirit of inclusiveness, it should be noted that some people do not have the ability to use their vocal cords yet nonetheless possess a very strong individual voice. Words are also an element of voice. We each have a unique use of vocabulary, syntax, style, and grammar—all of which relate to the words you choose and how you arrange them. Further, your voice is made up of insights, memories, stories, ideas, opinions, and facts with observations to back them up. Our voice expression is necessarily tied up in the language we use; multilinguals can relate to the experience of being able to be more expressive in one language than another. All of these are the raw material you draw on in expressing yourself. Just as you choose which words to use, you also choose which memories or ideas to use and which to hold back.

So much is communicated nonverbally through things like body language and gesture, both of which are, of course, culturally defined. These nonverbal components all contribute toward our overall "presence"—an elusive quality but one that really does come down to specific behaviors. The best leaders often have a distinctive presence.

You can think of all of these aspects of voice as a big toolbox. Unless we are trained speakers, we tend to use these tools instinctively not deliberately or consciously. Which isn't to say we can't, nonetheless, be skillful in our use of these tools. You might try stepping back once in a while and observing the mechanics of how you exercise your voice. Alter your delivery, your tone, your style, your syntax, your emphasis. See if your voice feels different. Observe how this difference registers with others. It's really very similar to how we experiment with the idea of a new look or new persona when we try on a new outfit. Have fun with it!

Consider the following sentence: Everything I need is within me.

Read it out loud six times, each time stressing a different word. Notice how the meaning changes. And that's just by using one tool—emphasis—from your voice tool kit.* This should give you a taste of how, by varying all of the different communication tools at your disposal, you can modulate your voice and the effect you have on others, and ultimately create meaning.

STATEMENTS AND QUESTIONS

Yet this is a book, and a book is unavoidably focused on words, so let's return to words and how we use them. I mentioned breaking complicated tasks into chunks. A useful way to do so with language (and how we use it to create our voice) is to see it in terms of two basic structures: statements and questions. Most basically, a statement is a sentence that ends with a period or exclamation mark. And a question is a sentence that ends in a question mark. This is a statement. Is this a question? Yes, it is. Here's another statement. And on and on we go. Statement, question, back and forth. Statements can be remarks, proclamations, beliefs, opinions, observations, facts. Questions can be open-ended, closed-ended, curious, leading; they can be requests, pleas, inquiries, or explorations.

One simple but revealing exercise I do with coaching clients is have them guess what a pie chart of their typical speech patterns would look like. (You might try this as well.) Most people realize they spend a lot of their day making statements and not taking the time to pause and ask a truly probing, curious, open-ended question—and then really listening to and considering the response. Most people who do this exercise

---

* In our workshops, we teach participants to use that sentence as a mindset. Imagine waking up every morning and saying this sentence six times, each time emphasizing a different word. If you did that each day, you would greatly boost your ability to make a positive difference in your world.

decide they need to rebalance that pie chart and make more room for questions. Effective use of your voice means you are balancing your use of statements and questions. If all you take away from this section is that basic principle, you'll change your voice (and your impact) dramatically.

One method for balancing statements and questions—specifically for doing so in the work of inclusion—comes from Derald Wing Sue, a professor of clinical psychology at Columbia University who studies racism and anti-racism. I have found his approach to using voice in the face of microaggression particularly valuable. He offers this script: "I know you didn't mean/realize this, but when you (comment/behavior), it is hurtful/ offensive because _____. Instead, would you be willing to (use different language or behavior)?"* I love this script because it is easy, empathetic, strong, and kind. It has a beautiful balance of statements and questions.

If we go deeper into this script, we find it follows a balanced syntax and uses statement, summary, and question. So now we've introduced a third element into our speech-pattern pie chart: *summary*. When you can summarize back what you heard the other person say, you give them the gift of being understood, which is a building block of inclusion. It is often a demonstration of empathy too, which we have seen to be a critical component of emotional intelligence.

Instead of a pie chart, we might conceive of Derald Wing Sue's script as a triangle. At the top or apex of the triangle is our first action: making a statement. Following the triangle down to the right to the next angle, we ask a question. If we ask a question, we must listen to the response, so the bottom line represents listening. The bottom left angle of the triangle

---

* Hannah Yoon, "How to Respond to Microaggressions," *New Yorker*, March 3, 2020. https://www.nytimes.com/2020/03/03/smarter-living/how-to-re-spond-to-microaggressions.html.

is summary: our restatement of what we have just heard.*

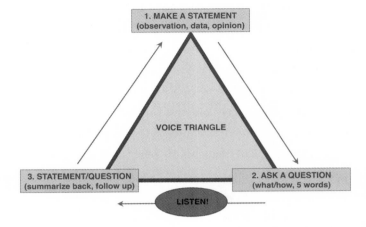

It just so happens that the triangle is considered by many to be the most stable geometric shape. I find this an incredibly powerful model for introducing greater balance and stability into how we employ our voice.

You might say, "Wait, doesn't this model have only one question and two statements?" Not really. Summary is almost always a mix of statement and question. Sometimes the question is explicit, as here: "It sounds like you're hurt by what your manager said about your work. Have I understood that right?" Even if there isn't a direct question, used properly, summary has the spirit of a question. We are checking with the other person to make sure we have understood them the way *they want* to be understood. We are inviting them to correct our summary or follow up and expand upon their point. Cycling through this sequence of statement, question, then summary is a wonderful and intuitive way to refine how we use our voice.

---

* Adapted from the triangle model used in HAVEN Human Assets's Productive Conversations module.

—

Let's illustrate the triangle, and incorporate some of the other points we've been discussing, by revisiting the story I opened the book with: five-year-old me standing at the periphery of our school gym, thinking I was going to be excluded from my kindergarten class photo until my teacher Mrs. Haley skillfully intervened.

First and foremost, Mrs. Haley employed deep and empathetic You listening. Listening isn't just hearing the words but observing and taking in the whole of a sometimes complicated group dynamic. It's reading the room. She noticed what was happening and was able to view both my exclusion *and* Sebastian's act of excluding through a lens of compassion.

Perceiving what was going on, Mrs. Haley immediately exercised her voice. She took action. Inclusive leadership (and leadership generally) requires that we combine good listening with an active voice. It is important to point out that there is a wide range of ways to actively use your voice. In our research at RoundTable, we have explored what images and symbols are evoked when people think of exercising their voice as an ally. People have brought up the iconic image of X González forcefully exhorting the crowd at the 2018 March for Our Lives following the shooting at Marjory Stoneman Douglas High School. That was indeed a powerful moment, but it's not necessarily a representative one when it comes to the effective use of voice. You might think that such moments would inspire us to act and speak up on our own; but they can also intimidate us. It was, however, a beautiful example of the use of authentic voice.

We can use our voice quietly, and no less powerfully, as Mrs. Haley did that day. She didn't reprimand Sebastian but was, in fact, just as empathetic with him as she was with me. When she turned to him and asked,

"Isn't this great that we get to sit together as a class?" she was continuing to employ both her voice and her deep listening to create a space of inclusion for all of us.

How might Mrs. Haley have employed the triangle to further explore the incident and offer Sebastian a lasting learning moment?

I imagine the conversation could have gone something like this:

Mrs. Haley: "Sebastian, it's so nice that we all get to sit together in this class picture." (Top of the triangle, statement.) "What do you think?" (Bottom right of the triangle, question.)

Sebastian: "Yeah, it's fine . . . it's okay . . ." (Bottom of the triangle, listening.)

Mrs. Haley: "I notice you're being a bit quieter than usual, but it sounds like you're okay. Have I understood that right?" (Bottom left of the triangle, summary with a statement followed by a question to check for understanding.)

Sebastian: "Yeah . . . it's a little weird to take our picture like this. I want to sit beside my friends."

Mrs. Haley: "I can understand that you want to sit beside your friends!" (Statement.) "What would make you feel more comfortable here?" (Question.)

Sebastian: "Maybe I can sit on your lap, too?" (Listening.)

Mrs. Haley: "Oh, I would love to have you on my lap as well—that's why I've got two legs! Come over here." (Summary followed by a statement in the form of an invitation. The triangle is complete.)

This imagined dialogue is a little cheesy, but I think you get the point. And it's important to note with this example in mind that using our voice isn't just a matter of asserting our opinion and making bold declarations. We can also use our voice (and our listening) to invite others to use their voices. In this way, we can both lead and include others. A more aggressive approach by Mrs. Haley might have succeeded in including me but alienating and shaming Sebastian. Instead, in this example, she skillfully used the triangle to encourage Sebastian to open up as well—to demonstrate that he was also seen by her and to attempt to make him feel more fully included. It was only by including him as well that she could create the opportunity for him to change.

29

ALLYSHIP AND ADVOCACY

In exercising her voice on my behalf, Mrs. Haley was acting as an ally—whether or not she thought about it with that term. In this sense, voice is not just the expression of opinions, thoughts, or feelings. It is an action. And in this case, it was undertaken by someone with relative power and privilege who used that position as a platform for creating greater safety and inclusion for someone facing exclusion.

We will explore what it means to be an ally, the degrees or stages of allyship, what a platform is and how to use it here and in later chapters. As we start out, however, it is important first to point out that inclusive leadership often begins small. It may not even look like leadership at all. A major theme of some of the stories that will be featured in part IV of the book is the power of a small act, where someone sees someone else being wronged, excluded, or slighted, and instead of opting for silence and comfort, steps up and does something about it.

Another important point to get straight at the outset: I wrote that Mrs. Haley was exercising her voice *on my behalf*. And in this case, that was true. I was a girl in kindergarten and wasn't equipped to handle this situation on my own. My own voice was in a very early stage of development. But when talking about adults, specifically in the workplace, it is not productive to think of speaking or acting on behalf of others—even though this is an easy trap to fall into, especially as you are first learning what it means to be an ally. If you try to use your voice on behalf of others, you may inadvertently take others' voices away or speak incorrectly. But when you speak on your own behalf, your impact is more powerful and change is more likely. In fact, Mrs. Haley spoke on her behalf too: "Isn't it great that *we* get to sit together?"

At its best, allyship is a symbiotic relationship. So instead of thinking about speaking *on behalf of* others, think of inclusive leadership as taking place *alongside* and *with* underrepresented colleagues. Allyship means you are taking on the struggles of oppression and discrimination as if they were your own. Opportunities for allyship occur in a particular moment when you recognize you have a tailwind; you can use that advantage to create change for people facing headwinds in that same moment, thereby creating change for yourself and more.*

Many of us first encounter the idea of a symbiotic relationship when we study what scientists call *mutualism* in nature and biology. These are arrangements where two or more species interact in a manner that benefits both. An oft-cited example is that between the sea anemone (which looks like a plant but is actually an animal) and the clownfish. Sea anemone trap their prey by secreting a toxin when an animal brushes one of its tentacles, paralyzing it. The brightly colored clownfish has evolved a protective mucus and is able to safely find shelter amid the sea anemone, and it pays its host back by attracting other fish. In another example, three-fourths of all flowering plants are pollinated by animals like bees, who as they forage flowers for their nectar, inadvertently pick up and

---

*   Which is why allyship requires deep emotional and cultural intelligence to understand your own tailwinds and headwinds, and those of others.

spread the flower's pollen. Two dissimilar species benefit, and depend on, one another's existence and support.

Similarly, in the mutualism of good allyship, everyone wins. We belong to the same species, but we bring very different histories and social identities to the table. When you speak up as an ally, we all benefit—not just the underrepresented person. You, as the agent with the tailwind, also benefit. In the workplace, the entire organization is better off when historic biases are addressed and every employee is able to thrive. Society at large benefits as well, just like the natural ecosystem is nourished by mutualism across various species. Inequality and injustice are a drag on our collective well-being. The ripple effects of allyship are far reaching and expansive.

So, the question is: How can you be an effective ally?

In late 2016, I started doing focus groups with clients to learn what they wanted to understand about allyship and leadership. The top concern people had was this: "How and when should I act as an ally?" People wanted to understand the platforms available to them at work; they were understandably concerned about what kinds of situations would be appropriate or inappropriate to speak up in; they worried that the particular organizational dynamics of their workplaces had implicit rules about allyship. In other words: allyship was perceived as a risky venture, especially at work, in the arena on which your career and livelihood depend.

As a result, people often held back. They knew the issue of inclusion was important and that the stakes were high. But sometimes it seemed easier to just say nothing at all and instead pursue activism privately at home and in the community. Participants vulnerably expressed that their jobs were on the line. They'd observed others being reprimanded, ostracized, shamed, reported to HR, or fired for speaking up, and they didn't want that to happen to themselves too.

I knew there was a better way, though; I knew that allyship could be more accessible. I worried that the word *allyship* had been associated with radical and political activism, that it conjured up images of opposition and resistance. My perspective is this: allyship is a collaborative, harmonious act that intentionally brings people together through small acts of courage. It is not aggressive or violent or adversarial; that is exactly the opposite of its intention. We can (and should) do it with warmth and kindness not anger or frustration or impatience.

There is an inherent tension at work here: injustice can make us upset. I understand the anger that fuels protests for basic human rights, for example. But protest is different from allyship. The act of allyship is not an angry one. It is a loving one, a peaceful one. It is one that might be fueled by anger but is delivered with kindness. The participants in my focus groups helped me to see that allyship has been gravely misunderstood. Above all, I think of allyship as an experience that is both strong and kind. Although, there is plenty of room for candor, at times uncomfortable candor. "Kind" is not the same as "nice."

All that said, there is also no getting around the fact that allyship can be difficult and presents us with challenging choices. Let's look at three situations where you might find yourself with the choice to be and act as an ally.*

1. When you have tailwinds, and you are among others with tailwinds.

2. When you have tailwinds and are with someone with headwinds.

3. When you choose to work for change at a systemic level.

---

* See page 96 for a working definition of the terms *agent* and *target*—both useful but imperfect terms.

TAILWINDS AMONG TAILWINDS

In this scenario, you have some degree of privilege, and a member of the target group is not present. So your leverage is that of using your privilege to influence another person with privilege.

Let's take a group of men playing golf on a Sunday. One of them makes a joking but offensive remark about the young women playing at the next hole, and you (as a man) perceive the remark to be sexist. What are your options?

You could say nothing at all and just move on with the game. What impact would this have? Another option is to say something. Remembering that effective allyship is speaking on your own behalf while also supporting and standing alongside the target population (in this case women),* you could address your friend directly and say, "I'm offended by that," or, "Would you have said that if she were here and could hear you?" or, "What makes you say that?" or, "Please do not make offensive comments about women. It's not funny."

You could also go deeper and use the triangle to initiate a productive dialogue like this:

> *You*: "I know you don't mean to be offensive and sexist, but when you make comments like that about women's bodies, you are objectifying and minimizing them. Would you please stop?" (Statement, followed by question.)
> *Him*: "C'mon, I was just joking around. You know I'm not sexist; that's a really strong word."

---

* First, you are not purporting to be speaking for someone else. Second, you are expressing a personal stake in the issue, even if you are not affected in the same way as a target.

You: "Sounds like you were joking and you don't see yourself as sexist. You're offended that I would call you sexist—is that right?" (Listen and summarize.)

Him: "Yes, exactly."

You: "I know you're a good person, and I don't want to see you as sexist either. We all make mistakes. That's why it's important that you don't make comments, even if you see them as jokes, about women's bodies. Would you be willing to reconsider?" (Statement, followed by question.)

Him: "Yeah, I can see this is important to you. I didn't mean to offend anyone. Thanks for letting me know."

In this case, the friend, after initially being defensive, was fairly open to feedback. He might have been even more defensive or aggressively doubled down and counterattacked. In this case, one option would have been to press on and continue a couple more cycles of the triangle. At some point, you could walk away. Now, you might be thinking that his more understanding response is unlikely. But when we offer grace to others, they typically mirror that same grace back—it's quite magical. I know it might seem unlikely, but let's consider the possibility that his grace and understanding is actually the more likely response. I say this because I've seen it over and over in my practice as a coach. It appears that grace invites reciprocity.

At some point, you could also boldly state your boundaries: "If you continue to be offensive toward women, I'll have to stop playing golf with you." Having a genuine and open conversation—one in which you attempt to empathize and show grace—can yield a change in attitude and ultimately behavior. This is how allyship can be at once so simple and powerful. (And difficult.)

TAILWINDS AMONG HEADWINDS

In this scenario, you have the same privilege you had in the first one, but the challenge is in a way trickier because a target of the discrimination is present. You must be careful not to speak for or attribute emotion or intent to them. Your aim is to speak *alongside with*, not *on behalf of*.

Let's stick with the golf scenario. This time, imagine you are a mixed-gender group of friends, and the same male friend consistently interrupts the women and (without their permission) steps in to coach them on their techniques. What can you do here?

"Dude, you're mansplaining."

"What makes you think Asha needs your golf advice?"

"This is the third time you've interrupted. I'd like to hear the rest of what Angie was saying."

"I notice you're only coaching the women and none of the guys. What's that about?"

Keep in mind my earlier point, and be careful to avoid the following:

"If Asha wanted your help, she would have asked for it." You're speaking on Asha's behalf, not your own. This minimizes Asha's voice and may misrepresent her true sentiments.

"I'm sure Angie would like to finish what she was saying and is tired of you interrupting her. Go ahead, Angie." This appears to be supportive, but Angie might feel she could have said that herself and doesn't need you to speak for her.

"All these women are excellent golf players, and maybe if you asked nicely, they could teach *you* a thing or two about golf instead of you inserting yourself constantly." First, do not volunteer women for their labor—that's up to them! Second, the statement doesn't express any empathy or support for the women dealing with the constant interruptions and mansplaining. It just compliments the women's golf skills, which could be perceived as condescending, misguided, and unsupportive.

INITIATING CHANGE AT THE SYSTEMIC LEVEL

Systemic change can seem daunting. If you take an incremental approach, you can start to see small wins that will motivate you (and others) to keep going.* Systemic change happens when we can look critically at policies and systems and change them to be more inclusive and equitable. As you move to initiate change, consider two questions: First, what are the pathways to change? Second, what are your platforms—your levers—for change?†

Let's take this as an example: you've noticed that the performance-review system seems to inherently benefit some people over others, either based on their identity or position. This is a perfect example where bias isn't a matter of individual actions or intent but is instead baked into the system. What can you do?

A good first step might be to express your concerns to Human

---

* Particularly in the corporate world, I lean toward emphasizing this incremental approach; it allows you to safely experiment and learn from small errors. But make no mistake, there are moments as well that do call for big, bold steps.

† We will look at platforms more closely in chapters 50 and 51 "The Power of One" and "The Power of Two"; but partnerships figure heavily in your ability to effect change.

Resources or your direct supervisor.* As you proceed, don't isolate yourself on an island. Build cross-functional partnerships with people who are likely to support change. Make it about teamwork and collaboration. Instead of seeking to be right (thereby making others wrong), seek to share, connect, and grow with others. Ask lots of questions and gather a lot of information. Seek evidence that contradicts your beliefs, keep in mind the wisdom of dissent, and be prepared to admit that you might be wrong. This is practicing inclusive team work, and it will create a stronger case for your plan.

It is essential that you be clear about your intention to engage in this work and that you share that intention with others. Fashion the sharing of your intention along the lines of an invitation as opposed to an assertion. Here are some ways you might, for example, get the ball rolling on enacting change in your company's hiring practices:

"I'm not sure we are reaching the full range of candidates. Let me explore this. Who wants to join me?"

"Has everyone had a chance to share? Who feels differently?"

"I'd like us to consider nontraditional candidates alongside the pool of candidates we already have. How can we do that?"

"What measures do we have in place to ensure that our hiring practices are equitable, just, and diverse? If we don't have those, who'd like to join me in exploring that question?"

---

* I say HR by way of example, but sometimes the best route is to informally approach a colleague. Keep in mind we all have both formal and informal means of influence. We can't distribute all personnel issues to HR, nor can we hold them accountable to solving them all; that can be a cop out.

A LEADER AND A FOLLOWER

Finally, I would be remiss if I didn't state the most obvious act of allyship available to us: to consider your own role as a leader *and* as a follower. Who do you follow? Who do you lead? When we ask our JEDI© participants these seemingly basic questions, people are surprised to see that they typically follow or are influenced by people who look like them or who have more social privilege than them. Similarly, they are often dismayed to recognize that, when they are in a position of privilege, the people who follow them tend to be from underrepresented groups.

Such long-standing patterns tend to support the status quo. Switching things up and consciously going against the grain of those patterns can be a powerful way to shake this up. Allow yourself to be led by underrepresented colleagues. Be mindful of how embedded privilege gives certain people more opportunities to lead. You will need to deliberately take on the mindsets of curiosity, humility, and relationship-building, and willingly be influenced by people you might not have considered to be leaders before—particularly anyone with less social privilege than you. It's one thing to support underrepresented colleagues; it's a whole other thing to be led by them. Create opportunities for your underrepresented colleagues to be leaders. Encourage them directly to lead, advocate for them (with their permission), and let them know that their voice matters and that you want to hear it and be led by them. This will require you to open your mind to new possibilities and ways of working in and seeing the world.

And if you are in the position of being underrepresented, you will need to exercise your leadership more deliberately—in psychologically safe environments—and in partnership with potential allies.

30

YOUR JOURNEY AS AN ALLY

We've talked about how a key inflection point in your evolution as an ally is when you realize the point of allyship is to speak up not on behalf of others but alongside them. As you've already read previously in these pages: allyship is taking on the struggle as your own. That's actually a big step forward. It's quite possible that, depending on your background, your own allyship might start with much smaller baby steps.

One useful framework for conceiving of our journey as allies is Jennifer Brown's Ally Continuum, which consists of five stages of progressive development.[*]

The first stage, which is more of a starting point, is being **unaware**. If you're reading this book, you're unlikely at that stage. Yet inclusive leadership involves awareness and action on multiple fronts. You might, for example, consider yourself fairly conversant with issues of gender equity but only just beginning to learn about neurodivergence. The term itself may be new to you. That's okay! Many of our mistakes occur when we bump up against things we didn't know, against the limits of our own

---

[*] Jennifer Brown, "From Unaware to Accomplice: The Ally Continuum," minisode #14, June 2018, in *The Will to Change*, podcast.

awareness. On every issue, we start out as a beginner.

With **aware**, the second stage, we begin to grasp the contours of an issue we had previously been unaware of or whose breadth we had underestimated. We can see the problem and the human impact it has. As your awareness grows, so does your curiosity. And, critically, you take it upon yourself to learn more without expecting those directly affected to do the teaching for you.

The third stage is when you put that knowledge into practice and you are now **active**. As we've discussed from the very beginning of the book, there is no perfect time to take action, no moment when our awareness suddenly crosses a necessary threshold and we become qualified to enter the fray. We have to take the leap and start taking chances sooner than later.

In Brown's framework, you move on to the fourth stage and become an **advocate** when you are not only active but proactive. You don't wait for others to act first and then step in and provide support. You raise issues and initiate difficult conversations. You hold people accountable.

The fifth stage, **accomplice**, is when you are willing to tackle systemic barriers to full inclusion and equity. For me, this term also captures that critical inflection point I mentioned earlier: when you develop such a personal stake in the struggle that it becomes your fight as well, a part of your own identity.

———

While the Ally Continuum is a useful framework, up to a point, it may seem at first glance that the development of allyship is a clear, linear progression—when in my experience, the reality is more complicated and messy. As we just discussed, one can be a seasoned ally on one question of inclusion and a total beginner in another. Even in areas where we might consider ourselves to be quite knowledgeable, we are always bumping up against the limits of our awareness and learning (often the hard way!) about something we had failed to see. In that sense, we continually find ourselves in the position of beginners. The journey is not linear but circular. Sometimes we lose the thread and go backward. Brown herself acknowledges this messiness. As I will share in part IV, some of my best and dearest clients have had (and continue to have) circuitous paths as inclusive leaders.

Additionally, the Ally Continuum is largely focused on behavior. Actions are important, of course. But that leap I've spoken of—when we're fighting alongside and not on behalf of others, when we have a deep personal stake in the cause of inclusion—is at the heart, a matter of identity. Perhaps it's the developmental psychologist in me, but I think the biggest shifts we undergo (and the biggest fears we face) on the path to being the ally and leader we want to be occur on the psychological plane.

The framework we've developed at RoundTable is less a journey and more of a psychological map: a way of making sense of the challenges and hurdles you will have to overcome (over and over) as you evolve in your role of what we call an ally-leader, a leader for whom inclusion and equity are at the core of their leadership journey.

I sometimes refer to the four steps as milestones or stages. But those terms are imperfect (as language often is!) as they imply a sequential, linear journey in which, like climbing a mountain, you ascend from one to the next, leaving the previous stage behind. Sometimes it may feel like this. At other times, it will feel more like a cycle, or a spiral, in which you repeat the steps over and over. But this repetition doesn't mean you're

L.E.A.D: IDENTITY JOURNEY OF THE ALLY-LEADER

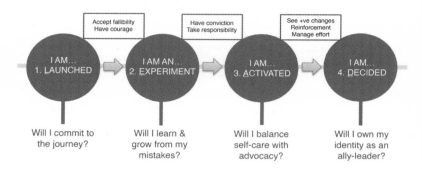

stuck; you are indeed making progress and ascending to higher levels of understanding and engagement. And at other times, you may feel as if you are in more than one mode simultaneously—more advanced in some ways but in other ways feeling the doubt and trepidation of a beginner. Each phase is marked by an essential tension you need to resolve before you can move on to the next one; and by some defining qualities you must cultivate in the process.

LAUNCHED

This is the "taking the leap" moment we talked about at the very beginning of part III. You feel inspired and committed but also unprepared. You finally understand the stakes, and that's a huge step. But those stakes feel really high, maybe overwhelming. You are not sure you are up to the challenge. This phase is therefore characterized by uncertainty, fear, and indecision. Your hesitation may be exacerbated by guilt (*Why haven't I done this sooner?*) or ambivalence (*How much do I really want to do this?*).

The psychological tension in this initial phase is clear: Are you committed to embarking on this journey? Are you ready to take the leap, knowing full well the risks entailed?

To make that leap, you must *accept your fallibility* and you must *have courage.*

EXPERIMENT

Throughout the book, I've urged you to experiment and embrace the prospect of making mistakes. In that sense, I used the word *experiment* as a verb. Here, I'm also using it as a noun. This is a framework that clarifies your evolving identity as an inclusive leader. And in this experience, you yourself are an experiment, a work in progress. As such, your mindset is not about success or getting it right; you are not going to be the perfect ally.

This mode is characterized by feeling ready to try things out and mess up. You understand that you're a work in progress, so you attempt to repair, sometimes give up, and try again, while remaining committed to making a positive difference, however inconsistently. You are taking ideas and principles you have learned in theory and trying them out in practice. It can be scary—your battle armor is on and you are receiving punches. You may even beat yourself up, be your own harshest critic. It's hard to mess up and keep going. Here, you are confronting who you are—your social identities, which as we've discussed, are multiple and evolving. And you are feeling the normal discomfort that comes with understanding your privilege or lack of privilege.

The psychological tension here is: Can I grow from my mistakes?

To do so, you must *have conviction* and *take responsibility.*

ACTIVATED

You've come a long way by this point. You have the necessary commitment to take the leap and enter the fray. You have the conviction to persist through your growing pains. You have learned to take responsibility for your mistakes and for the influence you wield. You're well on your way to becoming an effective inclusive leader. You still make mistakes but fully accept them as part of the process, even as you are making fewer of them. You are getting it "right" more often than you are getting it wrong; your actions yield positive outcomes for others more often and more consistently. Your errors are smaller.

Accordingly, you feel prepared and confident more often than not. Your guards are down, and you are better able to settle into the idea that allyship and inclusive leadership are part of your identity, of who you are. Yet you are still learning and growing. In particular, you are learning your limits and how to sustain yourself in this effort for the long term. You know the stakes are high, and you want to do all you can. An event in the news or in your company may have galvanized your passion. You want to go go go and push push push, because you see positive outcomes and you know real change is possible. That passion can lead to burnout as you learn your limits and how to pace yourself. There will be progress but also setbacks, and you may not be prepared for them. You may find yourself deflated and suddenly tempted to give up.

The psychological tension in this phase is finding the balance between *taking care of yourself* and *advocating for the cause of justice and equity*. Here, we learn that allyship doesn't mean constant and unrelenting action; it means consistent action coupled with reflection, pausing, and building support systems.

Weathering this critical stage of maturation requires several things: you must *see positive changes* from your efforts, *experience reinforcement* of your actions and beliefs, and learn to *manage your efforts and energy.*

DECIDED

With a track record of consistent effort and results over time, you are ready to stay in this effort for the long haul. You've cycled through being afraid and uncertain; questioning your commitment and capacity at times; recommitting, experimenting, learning, and growing; getting tired and giving up; and learning to act and engage consistently. You've solidified a necessary set of core skills: active listening and using your voice in productive and sometimes difficult conversations. Speaking up for justice and equity feels automatic, natural, and habitual (but can nevertheless still feel scary!).

Because this role is now part of your identity, and because your personality and life experience are unique, you have developed a signature style of leadership. Speaking up with your authentic voice feels necessary and maybe even natural, and you see it as a gift even as it, at times, requires courage. You are generous and gracious to yourself and to others, but you remain vulnerable to mistakes and to pain. You are doing it because it is who you are, not because it feels good or brings acknowledgment. You can actively prevent and reduce harm. You have become the calling. Other people are undoubtedly learning from your example, and you may be actively teaching it to others. The psychological aim here is to claim, own, and deepen this identity while not doubting who you are, where you've come from, and who you have become.

To stay on this long-term course, you must consistently see yourself as both a leader and an ally.

RELAUNCHING

That all seems straightforward (if not easy) on paper. As I've presented it, it may appear sequential and linear. Again, it can sometimes feel like that. But it gets complicated and confusing when we feel we've gone backward and have to start all over again, when we have come to see ourselves as a seasoned ally-leader but then encounter a crisis that challenges us in new ways and makes us aware of how much we still do not fully understand, when we realize we have to launch and experiment once again.*

Shortly before I wrote this chapter, I went through a kind of relaunch with a longtime client and his company. For a variety of reasons, some beyond his control, he had had to put his vision for DEI at his company (something he was deeply committed to from day one) on the back burner. With the company's business prospects now on more solid footing, he was ready to recommit. And so there we were, taking a largely new team through the JEDI© training, just as we'd done years ago. But it wasn't like we were starting over. We had our shared history. He had grown as a leader and better understood the challenges of being an inclusive leader in an industry not known for its diversity. Despite some ups and downs, he had built a culture of trust and loyalty. There was a lot to build on.

Many of our own journeys, individually and as organizations, will likely go through such a pattern of stop-and-start. We may, at times, feel we have lost the thread. But when we restart, all of those past efforts and lessons will be there as a kind of muscle memory we can draw on.

---

* Critically, going through that cycle again gets easier for the most part. You are familiar with the steps and the challenges. Identity is often a felt experience, so the feelings will be familiar. You know you have the tools. You've done this before. You've got this!

AUTHENTIC VS. PERFORMATIVE ALLYSHIP

I want to close this chapter with my interpretation of performative allyship and what I perceive to be a punitive narrative around the correctness of how we do allyship. It echoes a sentiment I see in my work and on social media all the time. I understand the frustration with seeing people post outrage about injustice on social media while the question remains if they are really doing anything constructive to make things better. In the corporate world, as I've mentioned before, a lot of companies issued strong statements about racial injustice in the weeks after George Floyd was murdered, but they didn't really put their money where their mouth was. They didn't walk the talk.

At times, the gap between stated intent and impact, between word and action, does come down to a kind of disingenuous virtue signaling, which needs to be called out. Hypocrisy is a real thing and detrimental to the cause.

But there are other times when that gap is simply part of human fallibility and of the growth process. Those small errors I am urging you to love are all about our intent not quite materializing as we'd hoped it would. We can fall short for *so many* reasons. We might underestimate the depth or nature of the problem, of the commitment we need to muster to be part of the solution, or of our own inherited biases. We might jump in with great enthusiasm, only to falter after a discouraging experience.

I worry that because people have been admonished for being performative, they will stop altogether. The accusation of being performative is, ironically, exclusionary. As much as I'm concerned about people doing harm in their allyship efforts, I'm also concerned that the language of performative allyship might exclude well-intentioned people from experimenting and learning from their mistakes . . . and ultimately doing good in the world.

Yes, we need to be thoughtful about our journey. Yes, we need to prevent harm and ensure that we are following through on our commitments. We need to "walk the talk." To me, that's what good leadership is.

I don't think the difference between authentic and "performative" allyship is nearly as clear or binary as some might suggest. Earlier I touched on the language we use to describe how we translate our inner selves into the social world: we say we *present* a given social identity or personality. It's a curious word, suggesting as it does an element of artifice or performance. We may wonder: How can a quality be real or authentic if it's being performed?

Yet think about your own evolution as a distinct person. When we are young, we try on different personas like costumes in a play. Role-playing is part of the process of discovering and experimenting with who we are. Faking it until you make it is a part of human development. When I first tried taking on the role of coach with the kids in my neighborhood, I had no idea what I was doing! I was making it up, borrowing drills from my swim coach, and mimicking things I'd seen the coaches and teachers I admired so much do. I was playacting; I was performing.

Early in your inclusive journey, you may find yourself borrowing phrases and techniques from more experienced leaders you admire. It may feel a bit like performing; you may doubt yourself and wonder if you're an impostor. But if you stick with it and practice honesty with yourself and vulnerability with others, you will find your own style and your own voice. The performance will become who you are.

31

THE STOP-AND-START CYCLE

When I looked at my notes about different clients, I noticed a pattern. I described one client's growth as an inclusive leader as "rapid but inconsistent." With another, I observed a stop-and-start cycle: a short burst of passionate commitment to the cause of DEI followed by a stretch of losing focus. This pattern of inconsistency, of taking two steps forward and one step back, is inherent to human development. And it can be especially pronounced in any difficult endeavor like the work of inclusion—where the cause is inspiring but the challenge steep and daunting. I wrote about companies who, galvanized by the injustice of George Floyd's murder, issued bold proclamations and commitments and then struggled to follow through. I wrote about the media company Axios encouraging its employees to speak out publicly about George Floyd only to later recant their position and refer to that period as a "fleeting moment of unity."

So what are we to do about this inconsistency? Should we tap the brakes early on to pace ourselves and prevent that initial enthusiasm from later faltering? Are there other steps we can take to mitigate against a stop-and-start pattern of progress?

I don't think so. I've said it before about mistakes and stumbles and losing our way: this is what human development looks like. It is typically not linear. We have breakthroughs and aha moments, and then we hit a wall or a speed bump or a plateau. We may even regress before regaining momentum. We need that early enthusiasm to ignite us and get us past our fears and doubts. Just because our commitment falters doesn't mean it's gone. We can revisit our original impulse to act and leverage it.

Moreover, it is often precisely when we are struggling with our own inconsistency and maybe doubting ourselves—Was my commitment sincere? Was I being performative? Am I truly up to the task of inclusive leadership?—that we learn the most. In these moments, we discover firsthand what gets in the way of change. We bump up against the enormous inertia of business as usual.*

I have one client who summarized a rough patch in his leadership journey in such a simple and lovely way. "Early on I was learning. Now I'm growing." The growth he spoke of emerged directly out of a period where he was frustrated with not being able to sustain the momentum of his early progress. He was dealing with regret and facing the fact that he had made mistakes. But he knew this difficult growth was necessary. And he correctly identified the next stage: recommitting and engaging in what he termed "decisive action."

Sometimes it helps to visualize that sense of reaching an impasse and bring it into the physical world as a concrete metaphor. If a client says they feel like they're hitting a wall, I'll say let's work with that. We'll step up to an office wall and imagine it as an imposing brick wall. What does it feel like to push against it, to sense its unyielding presence holding you back?

---

* One way you can build in greater consistency is by fully embracing and internalizing the idea of DEI as a business imperative, make it part of business as usual. When you don't 100 percent believe in the business case for inclusion, it will always be easy to put on the back burner.

Repeatedly, I have found that these moments of being stuck or at an impasse can be great teachers if you just stay with them and with the discomfort that comes with them. In fact, in many of our workshops, we teach a technique or mode called *stay*, and it is one I urge you to adopt as an inclusive leader with colleagues, employees, and mentees. For it to work, you have to set aside the impulse to help the person find a solution—which is not easy, because most business leaders are by nature fixers and problem solvers. But refraining from stepping forward to help or fix is itself a show of faith; you are showing them you believe they have the resources to work their way through this difficult stretch. With your belief and presence, they can rise to the moment. In a sense, it is an extension of dancing in the moment, learning to be in the midst of an uncomfortable situation without a clear agenda or path forward. More often than not, the act of staying with that discomfort generates a way out.

Creating a more inclusive workplace and a more just world is heady stuff. Let's for a moment examine the dynamics of the stop-and-start cycle with a slightly less loaded illustration. Say you're trying to lose twenty pounds, and in your early momentum, you quickly lose fifteen over the course of a few months. But you just can't seem to shake that final five pounds. In fact, you find yourself backsliding and putting on a few of those pounds you thought were gone forever.

This is an opportunity to recommit not just to your original goal but, perhaps more importantly, to the impulse behind that goal. You may even reappraise that goal and what really matters. Is it the number on the scale that matters? Or is it more about your energy and vitality?

Similarly, in the journey of inclusive leadership, the speedbumps (or brick walls!) you encounter may be a sign that it is time to reappraise or reframe. They are certainly *not* a signal to stop or slow down. Nor are they a warning that you got out of the gate too fast.

———

As you struggle with your own inconsistency and these crossroads where your early idealism bumps up against business imperatives or the resistance of business as usual, you may wonder whether you are guilty of performative allyship. As I wrote in the previous chapter, I don't believe in a rigid binary between "authentic" allyship and so-called performative allyship. Performing is often how we experiment with new tools, with new dimensions to our voice and our presence. It is like trying on a new outfit to see how it makes us feel, how we move in it. We may strike an awkward or false note in that new outfit. But that doesn't make us disingenuous. This, too, is what human development looks like. Sometimes we start with performance and only later (after we have fully absorbed this new part of ourselves) arrive at congruence.

———

One last thought on the stop-and-start cycle. I myself have moments where it's not so much that I am hopeless as that the way forward seems murky. "Am I really making any progress?" I ask myself.

Then, invariably, I will get an email from a client sharing a small moment. In one such instance, a client told me, "I found myself having a different kind of conversation with my neighbor about equity." Even if this doesn't seem like much, it encourages me. This is what human development looks like. A changed conversation leads to open minds. And open minds lead to new behaviors.

Our path may have stops and starts at times. Yet in truth, once we have launched our inclusive journeys, we never actually stop. We may not be moving forward in the way we had envisioned. But we are moving. That is the way of life.

32

CULTIVATING PSYCHOLOGICAL SAFETY

We ended part II with a discussion of why psychological safety is pivotal to and, in many ways, the "secret sauce" to a healthy organizational culture both in general and specifically to the work of inclusive leadership.

I hope the preceding chapters of part III have only bolstered my case for the importance of psychological safety. Speaking up on issues of discrimination, bias, and exclusion is not easy. We run the risk of saying the wrong thing (or, as we will discuss in chapter 37, the less-than-perfect thing). Identity—both our own and that of others—is a tricky and intimate subject. We won't "take the leap" and wade into these difficult waters unless we feel safe to do so. Remember, good listening goes hand in hand with the effective use of our voice. An organizational culture marked by psychological safety values and makes space for each and every voice. Listening is a foundational act in such an organization.

So how do we go about creating psychological safety in our organizations? Just as important, how can we maintain and deepen it? How do we know when it is running strong, and how do we know when it is waning?

This last question is critical because building psychological safety is not a one-off matter. It is not like physical infrastructure that, once in place, only needs a little cleaning and maintenance now and then. It is the psychological, relational infrastructure of your organization, and it must constantly be attended to. Think of it like a relationship. Falling in love is only the first step. Sustaining the relationship is an ongoing, long-term process of reading, listening, checking in, and deepening mutual understanding. Similarly, sustaining psychological safety in your organization will have its ebbs and flows. Keeping it healthy is like tending a garden.

———

"We are what we repeatedly do" is a pithy quote often attributed to Aristotle.* It's a good way of talking about how to create psychological safety in your organization. Recall that in Amy Edmondson's initial work with nurses, she found it was the informal, unofficial norms in psychologically safe units that set them apart. Attitude and intention help, but ultimate psychological safety is about behavior. Repeated behavior.

Most crucially, the behaviors I'm talking about are relational and interpersonal. They occur in the context of relationships, not in isolation. Psychological safety is a dynamic, which means that it happens within and between people. It is not a given; it must be developed, and it requires effort. So if you, as a leader and a team member, place a premium on building healthy relationships in the workplace, you will be well on your way to helping to cultivate psychological safety in your organization.

There are specific behaviors that go into building such healthy relationships. You must get to know your colleagues and coworkers in a meaningful way by listening to them and by asking questions that

---

* It's actually the writer Will Durant elegantly synthesizing a couple of observations from Aristotle.

demonstrate you are genuinely interested in them. Likewise, you need to meaningfully and authentically share who *you* are. Tell them what you did on the weekend; talk about your hobbies and family; take risks in being vulnerable. Additionally, you should demonstrate concern. Proactively ask how they are doing, show empathy, and ask how you can help.

Basically, you are calling upon all of the tools we discussed earlier—emotional intelligence, listening, and voice—and using those to build better, deeper relationships. This, in turn, will lead to psychological safety and trust.

FEEDBACK

Our observations and the literature suggest that being mindful of your *feedback practices* also goes a long way toward building psychological safety. Feedback is a very specific relational skill that is enormously important in the workplace. When we think of feedback at work, our first thought may be the formal feedback that supervisors and managers provide their direct reports. And of course that is important.

But what might be termed in-the-flow-of-work feedback is critical in its own right. Feedback is one of the core prerequisites for the "flow state" identified by psychologist Mihaly Csikszentmihalyi. One of the reasons sports are so conducive to flow is they provide immediate and clear feedback as to how we are doing. In a race, you can tell whether you are behind or ahead of your closest competition. In basketball, you know whether your form is correct when the ball either goes in the net or doesn't.

We need that moment-to-moment feedback at work as well, but we often don't get it. A majority of employees say they want to be "developed" in their jobs—they want clear, usable feedback to help them grow and improve. But only a third say they actually get the feedback they need.

A big reason for this gap is that feedback can be scary. Constructive feedback, which often has an element of criticism involved, can feel like a threat. We respond physiologically to perceived social threats just as we do to perceived physical threats. And that heightened fight-or-flight state doesn't lend itself to taking criticism well. A study by the NeuroLeadership Institute found that when someone actively *asks* for feedback, this defensive reaction can be significantly mitigated.[*] It's also easier on the person giving the feedback, as the request for feedback usually indicates what kind of feedback the person is looking for.

Asking for feedback can also help you avoid another pitfall: what psychologists call the "brittle smiles" phenomenon. This is when the one giving the feedback feels compelled to be "nice" and overcompensates instead of speaking clearly and candidly. Researchers measured heart rates during such exchanges and found that, while they may appear to be "friendly" on the surface, both parties were, in fact, feeling terribly anxious.[†]

Which brings me to another key point: psychological safety doesn't mean people aren't challenged. It's not about being "nice." Candid, no-bs feedback challenges people to step up their game and perform at a level you know they can achieve. That implicit belief in someone else—at times, you may believe in them more than they believe in themselves—can really build safety. When you believe in someone and confirm that belief with your words and actions, they will be more likely to take risks, be creative, and innovate. They know you will support them even if they mess up. Similarly, acknowledging and celebrating successes by sharing credit is

---

[*]   Cliff David and Barbara Steel, "How Focusing on Feedback Can Unlock Better Performance," NeuroLeadership Institute, November 5, 2020.

[†]   David Rock, Beth Jones, and Chris Weller, "Using Neuroscience to Make Feedback Work and Feel Better," *Strategy and Business*, no. 93 (August 27, 2018). https://www.strategy-business.com/article/Using-Neuroscience-to-Make-Feedback-Work-and-Feel-Better.

critical to building psychological safety. People want to know that they are valued. Intentionally celebrating wins and acknowledging individuals for their efforts and results goes a long way in building safety.

MICRO-AFFIRMATIONS

We talked earlier about the debilitating effect of microaggressions. The positive parallel is *micro-affirmations*—nonverbal and verbal gestures that demonstrate concern, care, and encouragement. Nods, smiles, word choice, and check-ins are examples. Shout out to the people who smile and nod at us when we are on stage performing: those people are affirming us and offering us safety.

While we're on the topic, it's important to point out just how fragile psychological safety is and how quickly it can be eroded (often unintentionally) by opposing behaviors—like those aforementioned microaggressions. Other corrosive behaviors include unequal participation, favoritism, blame, defensiveness, and various forms of passive-aggressive behavior.

Those are fairly obvious examples of behaviors that can create a sense of psychological *unsafety,** although their expression can sometimes be subtle and insidious. Yet there are more nuanced instances as well. For example, how you react when someone has an emotional episode at work

---

* Emotions may be universal, but how we express them is not. Likewise, it is important to keep in mind that there is no universal standard here. What may feel safe to me (e.g., someone smiling and asking about my day before we get down to work) may not feel safe for someone who is made excruciatingly uncomfortable by small talk. Because we can never know for sure, the key is to build relationships and trust with people so they can tell us what they need and what makes them safe (or unsafe), and we can ask.

can affect safety. When someone cries at work, do you get visibly uncomfortable, somehow communicating that this isn't a safe place to cry? Or do you yourself hold back tears (or cry with them), express concern, and lean into them in a way that shows it's okay to cry?

CLAIMING YOUR OWN PSYCHOLOGICAL SAFETY

A running refrain in this book has been that the emotional intelligence required for inclusive leadership involves paying attention to and taking care of your own needs as well. This certainly applies to psychological safety. What constitutes safety varies a good deal from person to person. What do *you* need to feel safe? Answering and acting on this question is important. Unless you tend to your own psychological safety, you won't take the necessary risks, show the necessary vulnerability, or extend the full generosity of spirit to others that great inclusive leadership demands. If you talk explicitly about your own safety and name what you need to feel safe, you will be modeling that same behavior for others.

When you know what you need, you can ask for it. *And* you can find it in places and relationships where your safety is already well established. Finding psychological safety was a long journey for me. Growing up in an Indian immigrant household in Canada, I was constantly wary of how people saw me, how I smelled, how I dressed. On top of the explicit bullying I experienced in school were offhand remarks that may have not been intended maliciously but stung and sharpened my self-consciousness of being different and other. I remember a girl who sat down next to me in the cafeteria and then moved away. "Eww, your clothes stink of Indian food," she said.

Those kinds of interactions left me hyperalert to anything I might say, do, wear, or eat that would underscore my Indianness. Moreover, my preoccupation prevented me from performing at my best in school. I had a habit of making excuses for who I was, minimizing or even blatantly lying about inherently Indian qualities I had. When you're doing that much emotional work to hide parts of yourself and simply be accepted, you can't possibly have enough psychological bandwidth to be the best person you can be academically and socially—much less to demonstrate concern over others' sense of belonging.

I never did feel psychologically safe at school. What I needed was to be seen, maybe even celebrated; for my Indianness to be acknowledged as a beautiful thing, instead of a disgusting thing. There were misguided attempts to celebrate my Indianness, but they actually did more harm than good. Like when my fourth-grade teacher asked my mom to come to school on Halloween wearing a sari, proclaiming that she "just loved Indian costumes." (Saris, of course, are not our *costumes* but, rather, every-day wear in India.)

Over the years, I've learned how to build the kind of environment I need to thrive and to recognize that I can't simply rely on others to do that. I've built partnerships and good friendships with potential allies, people who have demonstrated kindness, open-mindedness, and grace. I am getting better at asking for what I need. I will, for example, open a meeting by saying, "Can we take a moment to check in with each other before we get to the business part of the agenda?" Or I'll say, "Let's make sure we all ask one stupid question during this meeting," which is a brilliant practice that unearths assumptions, lowers the waterline, and dismantles the fear and necessity of courage to ask a question. Such practices not only tend to my own psychological safety but open the door for others to do so as well. Sometimes we don't know what we need until we don't have it. Being aware of how you're feeling in certain rooms can go a long way in helping you to understand what you need.

One final word on belonging and psychological safety. We tend to think of belonging as a welcome that others extend to us. And that *is* an element of belonging. But as I learned the hard way, I had to make a point of crafting my own sense of safety, of carving out the spaces where my sense of belonging was not in question. Sometimes we have to be bold and just *claim* belonging. In her MasterClass on writing for TV, Shonda Rhimes implores us to belong in every room we enter, at every table we are at.* She invites us to take the seat and not wait for someone else to determine if we belong or not. Although I have some reservations about this as a blanket strategy, the boldness of her challenge is healthy for those of us who don't find it easy to enter into a room and assume we belong—who may be inclined to look to others for permission or assurance.

I know that, for me, *not* assuming I belong everywhere heightens my awareness of how meaningful that small gesture—a nod of encouragement, an extra note of welcome in my voice—might be for others. But I also recognize that we have to take our belonging and sense of psychological safety into our own hands whenever we can.

---

* Shonda Rhimes, "Shonda Rhimes Teaches writing for Television," MasterClass series, accessed June 25, 2023. https://www.masterclass.com/classes/shonda-rhimes-teaches-writing-for-television.

33

EMOTIONAL INTELLIGENCE: RECONSIDERED

The chapter title here may puzzle you as I've already written two chapters about the importance of emotional intelligence. Indeed, for most of us in the business world, the proposition that cultivating the qualities associated with emotional intelligence is a worthy goal has become an article of faith, a self-evident given. It is especially so in the two areas in which I operate, coaching and inclusive leadership, where being self-aware and smart with our emotions is critical.

However, a sharply observed essay by Merve Emre in *The New Yorker*, "The Repressive Politics of Emotional Intelligence," gave me pause.* Emre's analysis of Daniel Goleman's decades of work espousing the virtues of emotional intelligence expands on what she perceives as a biased view of emotions and has made me reconsider my language and approach to this aspect of inclusive leadership.

As a point of reference, the standard definition of emotional intelligence goes like this: the capacity to be aware of, control, and express

---

* Merve Emre, "The Repressive Politics of Emotional Intelligence," *New Yorker*, April 19, 2021.

one's emotions, and to handle interpersonal relationships judiciously and empathetically. So far, so good. (Mostly.) When we are attuned to our own emotional state, we can make conscious, mindful decisions about how to handle whatever it is we are feeling in a given moment. When we do so, we also tend to be better (and more empathetic) at reading the emotions of others and in assessing the overall mood of the room. All of this equips us to be more sensitive and skillful in how we interact with others.

In my own work, the most common strategy by which I deploy emotional intelligence, as I understand it, is through what I call "observe and name." If a client says something that puzzles me, I will come out and say it. "I notice I am confused by what you've just said. Can we explore this further?" In a workshop, if I am not getting the participation from the group I was hoping for, I will come out and say it. "I'm observing that people aren't sharing their personal leadership challenges. What do you want to do about this?" If I sense discomfort during a discussion, I will note that. "It suddenly feels tense here. Have I got that right?"

I am not doing this to be provocative or to call people out. My intent is always to lower the waterline, to call attention to the unspoken, to bring what is hidden and obscured out into the open. It is not just that acknowledging the unspoken is healthy in and of itself (which it is). More often than not, the tension or discomfort I observe and name becomes the fuel that allows us to move forward, go deeper, and learn from one another.

As Fred "Mister" Rogers was fond of saying: "Anything that can be mentioned can be managed." I like the intent here, and Mister Rogers was actually very skilled at observing and naming. But his quote inadvertently points to the problem with EI. It's that last word: *managed*. Especially in the context of the workplace, that verb carries overtones of power and of the old (and now largely outdated) model of command-and-control management. Another verb that sometimes comes up with regard to emotions is *regulate*, which has those same overtones.

This theme of control is inescapable in Emre's essay. Her take is that emotional intelligence can be and has been used as a form of corporate control. It's not that we don't need to exercise a degree of self-control. We do. But I don't think of my relationship to my emotions in terms of control. I seek to work *with* my emotions, and with those of others, rather than *over* them. Just as, as a business owner, I seek to work *with* rather than *over* my employees. Yes, I am their boss, but I think of myself as working in partnership with them not as managing them.

In Goleman's world of managed emotions, there seems to be little room for anger and outrage. Or for justice. His unit of analysis is the individual. As I read Emre's essay, I found myself thinking of one of the most consistently powerful exercises in our JEDI© workshops: when we discuss the scenario of a Black employee overcome with grief and anger over the murder of a young Black man in their city, and not getting the support they need from their supervisor. Yes, the supervisor expresses empathy, up to a point. But they then stress that this is not a workplace issue and that the employee must compartmentalize in order to get on with the job at hand. In essence, the supervisor is asking that Black employee to be better at managing their emotions.

Additionally, when we talk about emotions, particularly emotional awareness, we must not neglect the various experiences of neurodivergence that can make it challenging or impossible to regulate, manage, or recognize emotions.

The most fruitful moments in my coaching, whether one-on-one or in group sessions, are almost always those when people stop managing complex emotions and tamping them down. When raw emotion spills out, uncensored, and things get a little messy and maybe uncomfortable. When we lower the waterline, we feel we have permission to stop regulating our thoughts and emotions.

We can't always be so vulnerable and candid. There are certainly moments when we need to be judicious and exercise restraint. But in general, I think the workplace needs more candor and vulnerability, not less. More messy conversations and fewer managed ones.

I certainly don't assume that the undercurrent of control Emre finds in Goleman's work is present in every conversation about emotional intelligence. I will continue to use the term as a helpful shorthand for a set of qualities I feel are essential in the workplace. But I will also be more mindful of—and ready to push back against—any attempt to use the concept to invalidate the healthy expression of anger and other raw emotions.

WOMEN'S ROLE IN EMOTIONAL LABOR

In her essay, Emre also asks whether we should be talking about emotional *labor* instead of emotional *intelligence*. The term *emotional labor* was first popularized by the sociologist Arlie Russell Hochschild in her 1983 book *The Managed Heart*.* Emotions play a part in virtually all human interactions; therefore, one would expect most kinds of work to involve a degree of emotional exertion. But Hochschild observed that professions requiring a high level of emotional labor (she cites flight attendants as one potent example) tended to be predominantly female and lower paying than male-dominated professions. Moreover, women in such professions were often expected to project a public emotion at odds with their private emotion (a flight attendant forcing a smile with a rude passenger). So women were getting the short end of the stick in more ways than one: having to adopt a forced public

---

* Arlie Russell Hochschild, *The Managed Heart* (Berkeley: University of California Press, 1983).

persona and being compensated less for doing so.

More recently, the term *emotional labor* has come to be used just as often in the context of relationships. One current definition of emotional labor is: the effort involved when a person takes on the responsibility to manage feelings and emotions in order to maintain a relationship, job, status, safety, or reputation. But Emre brings the term back to its original context in the workplace and raises the provocative question of whether EI has become a new form of emotional labor—a de facto requirement of the job in which women are expected to bear a disproportionate burden and for which they will be insufficiently rewarded and recognized. For anyone who feels the need to hide who they are—be it their culture, gender, language, sexual orientation, accent, etc.—this emotional labor becomes even more pronounced.

The last two *Women in the Workplace* reports by McKinsey and LeanIn.org suggest there is something to this.[*] On the one hand, the reports find that women are stepping up and doing the invisible work of fostering inclusiveness and overall well-being in the workplace. This is exactly the kind of leadership the COVID-19 pandemic revealed to be so essential to organizational health, leading to, among other things, higher retention rates and employee satisfaction. An analysis of the 2021 report in the *Harvard Business Review* broke out some of the many forms this work takes: helping employees navigate work-life challenges, ensuring manageable workloads, providing emotional support, speaking up against bias and championing diversity, and spending time on DEI work outside of their formal job responsibilities.[†]

---

[*] LeanIn.org, *Women in the Workplace.*
[†] Marianne Cooper, "Women Leaders Took on Even More Invisible Work During the Pandemic," *Harvard Business Review*, October 13, 2021.

Yet this work is far too often going unrecognized and unrewarded. Some 40 percent of women leaders say their DEI work isn't acknowledged in performance reviews. "Spending time and energy on work that isn't recognized could make it harder for women leaders to advance," the 2022 report observes. As a consequence, women in leadership are likely to be stretched thinner than men: 43 percent of women leaders say they are burned out compared to only 31 percent of men.

Talking about emotional intelligence as a kind of emotional labor reminds us of several important truths: EI is actual *work*; it is not just about individual attributes but about relationships, and those relationships happen in the context of an organization with a hierarchy and power dynamics. This latter point is key. The whole enterprise of inclusive work is built on the premise that organizations have biases and inequities built into them. So the question becomes: Who is expected to do the work of emotional intelligence? And who is recognized and rewarded for that work?

The term *emotional intelligence* (whatever its imperfections) has come to be an umbrella for a set of relational skills that are increasingly valuable in today's workplace, and that can be deliberately taught and cultivated in individuals and organizations. I don't wish to lose sight of that by asking these larger questions. But, like any aspect of organizational culture, the idea of emotional intelligence can take on and reflect long-standing biases and inequities. We have to bring a critical, curious, and inclusive lens to how it plays out in our work.

——

The discussion of who is performing the labor of emotional intelligence also begs the question: If some employees and leaders—very often women—are stepping up and doing more of their share of the invisible work that contributes to inclusive and thriving cultures, are others doing less than their share, less than they might?

To explore this question, we turn to a term that, like emotional labor, has come to be associated largely with relationships and the domestic sphere but which is equally applicable to the workplace: *weaponized incompetence*. Sounds ominous, doesn't it? The more folksy definition is simply this: when someone (in the context of relationships and house-work, almost always a man) feigns incompetence at a task (say, loading the dishwasher) and either avoids it or bungles it so completely that a woman decides it's easier just to keep on doing it herself. The term exploded when a woman posted a grocery list for her husband that included pictures of the items and a meticulous hand-drawn map of the store. The post was in jest, but it went viral and clearly struck a chord.*

We can see the same dynamic in the workplace as well. Says Melanie Ho, author of *Beyond Leaning In: Gender Equity and What Organizations are Up Against*, "In a previous job, I had a group of female coworkers where we'd joke about our 'gendered task of the day' every time we did something that wasn't an official responsibility but that women did to disproportionate extent."† Sometimes these are tasks traditionally associated with emotional labor and traditionally gendered—like the story of the woman who became the default organizer of employee-appreciation events. Other times, they are more technical tasks like operating the copy machine or properly formatting a legal document.

The term *weaponized incompetence* suggests conscious intent, which

---

* One reason it resonated so much during the pandemic is, despite the fact that both men and women were often working from home, gender disparities in household work and chores remained stubbornly persistent.
† Melanie Ho, *Beyond Leaning In: Gender Equity and What Organizations are Up Against* (Strategic Imagination, 2021).

I think both is and isn't true. Are men scheming to get out of certain responsibilities in a calculated way? Probably not. But neither are these behaviors entirely unknowing. There's a YouTube tutorial for *everything* now. If you want to figure something out, you will. In the end, these default, highly gendered divisions of labor are an easy way out.

And speaking of an easy way out . . . I've noted several times my impatience for a preemptive disclaimer I sometimes hear at the start of a workshop: "What can I really say about bias? I'm just a middle-aged white guy." Again, I don't think this is a calculated attempt by the speaker to absolve himself of responsibility. And I'm willing to give him the benefit of the doubt and acknowledge that this is partly a sincere show of humility.

But c'mon. Bias and inequity are part of the fabric of life. If you follow the news, if you pay attention to what happens around you, you've witnessed examples of people being dismissed or outright disparaged for their identity. We've all seen bullying in school and on the playground growing up. We all have mothers and know the unlevel playing field women face. It's fine to be humble and acknowledge you have a lot to learn. It's often a wise move to listen first. But there's no excuse for sitting on the sidelines.

Inclusive leadership—and the skill set of emotional intelligence it so heavily draws upon—is emotional labor. As with any form of labor, we should honor it, be mindful of how we divide that labor, and deliberate in how we recognize and reward it.

34

HOW WE PRESENT EMOTIONS

One final topic I want to consider in relation to emotional intelligence is the nuanced one of how we choose to project our internal emotional state into our relationships with others. You will note that we often talk about *presenting* a certain social identity, and I use that word here as well. In both cases, there is a complex interplay between *inter*personal (between people) and the *intra*personal (within ourselves) emotional dynamics. Our emotional state is not steady and fixed but constantly in flux.

We all know about "self-talk"—the running dialogue we have with ourselves. Our internal conversations spill over into our conversations with others, and vice versa. That internal conversation can be fraught with tension and unresolved issues. Our internal sense of self and the persona we present to others may, at times, feel aligned. More often than not, however, there is usually a slight dissonance or disconnect between the two. The mix of alignment and dissonance will change from situation to situation depending on our state of mind, the context, and many other factors. In some situations we may feel comfortable, for the most part, being our full, authentic selves. In other situations, with other people, on other days, we may be more guarded.

That dynamic applies to our social identity and to our emotions. In fact, the two are very much linked. Culture and social norms can exert considerable influence over how people of a given identity express emotion or are *expected* to do so. As a woman, I am cognizant of the fact that women are seen as inherently more emotional. Women leaders have to take those expectations into account all of the time. Whatever our identity, we can find ourselves internalizing inherited expectations without even being fully aware that we are doing so.

There is also a good deal of cultural variation in how people express emotions. In fact, experts disagree over just how universal human emotions are. For her book *Between Us: How Cultures Create Emotions*, psychologist Batja Mesquita surveyed people from around the world as to what does or does not constitute an emotion.[*] Interestingly, not all languages even have a word comparable to *emotion*. In some cultures, people were more likely to name behaviors than emotional states: laughing rather than joy, and crying rather than sadness. In such cultures, yelling and helping might be listed as emotions. She eventually came to the conclusion that emotions are as much relational as they are inner states, taking place as much *between* us as *within* us.

In other words, emotions live in the "third entity" I have talked about before. Which means that how emotions are expressed, muted, or avoided is very much dictated by context. As inclusive leaders, we need to be mindful of the relational dimension of emotions, of how fluid they can be. We have to guard against ascribing fixed or assumed emotions to others. We have to be aware of how cultural norms come with baggage and bias as to how and when people can display a given emotion.

---

* Batja Mesquita, *Between Us: How Cultures Create Emotions* (UK: WW Norton, 2022).

To bring the conversation full circle, we should also be aware of how the very notion of emotional intelligence as a kind of received wisdom in the workplace can become its own set of norms, prescribing certain ideas about what it means to be authentic with others. People can express qualities like warmth or empathy in very different ways. We have to be open to a diversity of emotional styles—especially as we learn more about the full range of neurodivergence. And when we're in doubt as to how to read someone, we can simply ask, however awkward that might feel.

As you know by now, I'm distrustful of playbooks. The research and teaching around emotional intelligence offers us enormously helpful tools for building relationships and creating inclusive and safe organizational cultures. But we shouldn't let it harden into a kind of dogma. Emotional intelligence can and should be more dance than dogma, fluid and evolving and subject to change.

Earlier, I posited EI as a precondition for the creation of psychological safety. In theory, I still believe that. But if we allow EI to become overly prescriptive—dictating how and when people should express certain emotions, or even dictating the very idea of emotional availability as a given in the workplace—then it is no longer fostering psychological safety, the freedom to be our full and authentic self, but limiting it.

35

UNCONSCIOUS BIAS

If psychological safety is a prerequisite to inclusive leadership, unconscious bias can be a snake in the garden undermining it. On the one hand, unconscious bias (in the sense in which it's usually used) is not a good thing and clearly has negative—if unintended—consequences for women, people of color, people with disabilities, the LGBTQIA+ community, and others. On the other hand, we shouldn't be so quick to demonize the unconscious bias we see in others or in ourselves. Let me explain.

To an extent, at least some of our unconscious bias is the byproduct of certain hardwired tendencies and preferences the human brain has developed over the process of evolution. I say *to an extent* because, over the course of human history, these ingrained tendencies have become intertwined with systems of privilege, exclusion, and oppression. And it would be wrong to say we are hardwired to be racist or sexist. But the quirks of the human brain do come into play, and understanding how this works can help us better mitigate their consequences.

A groundbreaking work in this vein is Daniel Kahneman's *Thinking, Fast and Slow.* Kahneman changed how we think about . . . how we think.

---

* Daniel Kahneman, *Thinking, Fast and Slow* (Farrar, Straus and Giroux, 2011).

Although he is a psychologist, his work had so many far-reaching implications, it would go on to win the Nobel Prize for Economics and is credited with helping to create the field of behavioral economics.

Kahneman's core insight is that the human mind has two modes: a slow, deliberate, conscious one; and a fast, intuitive, unconscious one. The second, quicker mode has been instrumental in helping us to survive, and its judgments are often remarkably sound. But its use of shortcuts leaves it vulnerable to error and bias.*

The brain's preferences and tendencies can't be wished away. We have to work with them, or in some cases, prevent them from working against us. Cognitive bias is here to stay. And to the extent that cognitive bias makes us vulnerable to cultural and other biases, bias generally is here to stay. We just have to be aware of it and work to mitigate its harmful effects.

We'll get to those efforts at mitigation (and what works and what doesn't work) in a minute. First let's zero in on two of the human brain's core tendencies. The brain loves patterns, and it also has a distinct preference for the familiar. The two are closely related. The brain is a pattern-spotting and pattern-making machine. It is through identifying patterns that we make sense of the world. We use patterns to create narratives that help us understand the past and anticipate the future, and to construct models for how the world works. (The sun rises in the east and sets in the west.) The human brain will see patterns even when none exist. Give a person three unrelated facts in succession, and they will begin crafting a story that links those three facts.

---

* When Kahneman and other psychologists talk about "cognitive bias," they're not using bias in the same way we do when we talk about racial or gender bias; it is more about the brain's preferences. So, in fact, we make decisions all of the time based on what might be called unconscious bias.

So yes, this tendency to see patterns has a significant downside and leads to errors. It has also helped us survive. The same is true of our preference for the familiar. Our primitive brain (which is still with us, largely intact) instinctively puts everything we encounter into one of two categories: either this is safe for me or it's a threat to me. The unfamiliar is unknown and possibly carries higher risk. The familiar is a known entity. (I have eaten this berry before, and it didn't kill me.)

Again, we are not hardwired to be sexist, racist, or any -ist for that matter. But when we encounter something or someone new or unfamiliar (and that can include a person of a certain race or ethnicity), we attempt— often clumsily or crudely—to relate them to what we already know. The result can be a stereotype, or at the very least a caricature. You might think of it as the brain's rough first draft at understanding something unfamiliar. We saw this dynamic play out in chapter 21 with the Apu character in *The Simpsons*. As a first introduction of a severely underrepresented (nearly invisible!) South Asian community into mainstream television, Apu was somewhat of a breakthrough. The problem is that this "first draft" understanding never evolved into something deeper.

Knowing that general cognitive bias—and specific unconscious bias based on social identity—operates at a deep level, often beyond the reach of conscious intent, has implications for how we try to address unconscious bias in the workplace. Companies spend millions (maybe billions) of dollars every year on some version of what is variously called diversity training, unconscious-bias training, and implicit-bias training.* The thinking here is that by bringing the workings of unconscious bias out of the shadows and into the light, we can, to some extent, disarm it.

It is all very well-intentioned. And taking the IAT can be a fascinating exercise. But, alone, such awareness-raising practices have been proven to be ineffective—and even to backfire. There is a phenomenon called "moral licensing" in which, when we engage in activity we think of as good behavior (like participating in a diversity-training session), we later cut ourselves some slack to do just the opposite. Iris Bohnet, a behavioral economist at Harvard, first acknowledged this phenomenon in her 2016 book *What Works: Gender Equality by Design.*† The book raises a lot of doubts about the efficacy of diversity training, and other research has confirmed her assertions. A 2019 meta-analysis of more than 490 studies found that unconscious-bias training did not change biased behavior. And an earlier study of 700 companies found that the likelihood of Black men and women advancing after unconscious-bias training actually *decreased* in many organizations.‡

So, what to do? As I indicated earlier, bias is stubborn because it operates out of sight. One strategy that Bohnet pushes in her book is to target the unconscious *behavior* that springs from unconscious bias. In works like the popular book *Nudge*, behavioral scientists advocate what they call

---

* The latter is based on an implicit association test (IAT) developed by social psychologists Mahzarin Banaji and Anthony Greenwald and summarized in their book *Blindspot: Hidden Biases of Good People.*

† Iris Bohnet, *What Works: Gender Equality by Design* (Cambridge, MA: Harvard University Press, 2016).

‡ Patrick Forscher et al., "A Meta-analysis of Procedures to Change Implicit Measures," *Journal of Personality and Social Psychology* 117, no. 3 (September 2019): 522–559.

"choice architecture"—altering the environment to "nudge" us to better choices.* For example, redesigning the order and display of food in a school cafeteria is a better way to get kids to eat healthier than by telling them to do so. As another example, replacing unstructured interviews and performance reviews with highly structured ones turns out to be an incredibly effective way of reducing bias.

Bohnet cites a fascinating example of a small design tweak that can reap significant results. In 1970, only 5 percent of the musicians in the nation's top orchestras were women. Having musicians audition from behind a screen increased the likelihood that a woman would advance to the next round by 50 percent. Today, women account for over a third of orchestra membership.

The other approach is to accompany implicit bias training with "prejudice-habit-breaking" training. Participants learn about how implicit bias works but then focus on practical strategies for minimizing bias in actual behavior. These strategies consist of exactly the kinds of activities and key behaviors we teach in JEDI:© calling out and naming stereotypical views, being curious about who people are as individuals beyond their perceived identity, reflecting on counter-stereotypical examples, learning to adopt the perspectives of others, and diversifying your interactions and networks. Researchers who studied these types of training have found that, even two years after participating in a workshop, students who had participated were more likely to speak out against bias than students who had not.[†]

---

* Richard H. Thaler and Cass R. Sunstein, *Nudge* (New York: Penguin, 2009).
† Patrick Forscher et al., "Breaking the Prejudice Habit: Mechanisms, Time-course, and Longevity," *Journal of Experimental Social Psychology*, no. 72 (2017): 133–146.

As I've said throughout this book, keep your focus on behavior and on relationships. Everything else springs from that.

36

THE LABORATORY OF REAL LIFE
(EXPERIMENT, EXPERIMENT!)

Your best lever for organizational change is to try to effect incremental shifts in behavior, especially in your most immediate relationships: the one-on-one interactions you have on a daily basis; the people you regularly sit around a table with. Behavior stems from the mindset you consciously choose. If you choose the mindset of "helpful," for example, you are going to behave differently than if you choose the mindset of "helpless." You can choose your mindset, which means it's a good place for you to invest if you want to change your behavior. But changing behavior, even in small ways, can be scary. It is one thing to sit through leadership training and nod in agreement at how you are now able to see the world in a different light. It is another thing to actually try to *be* different in the world.

And here again, psychological safety comes in. You and your team will be much more likely to take the leap and try altering and adjusting your behavior if you are surrounded by a culture of trust, vulnerability, and risk-taking.

And—perhaps somewhat paradoxically—you will feel even safer if you approach this process of tweaking behavior as an experiment.

The word *experiment* might initially make you nervous. Experiments go wrong, don't they? It depends on how you measure success. In the scientific world, the point of experiments isn't to get things right, especially not the first time. The point is to learn. The point is to collect data, analyze it, draw conclusions from it, and then see if the results can be replicated. In the world of science, that data is often quantifiable. In the world of work, that data is reflected in changes in the room and in your relationships that occur when you modify your behavior. Your laboratory in the workplace is the third entity we talked about earlier: that fluid, dynamic space between people. If I choose behavior *y* instead of my customary behavior *x*, how do people respond differently to me? How does that third entity shift? Does the energy of the room feel different?

You will recall the breakthrough moment in my own development as a coach and a leader when a co-facilitator and I agreed to go entirely off script in the workshops we were leading. It felt very much like an experiment at the time and a bit of a high-wire act. It was essential to have a trusted, open-minded, and open-hearted colleague to experiment with.

Trial and error is at the heart of the scientific method, and I encourage you to embrace that approach (and its inherent tolerance of risk and mistakes) in your work as an inclusive leader. Trial and error is also at the heart of all evolutionary change. It is the engine of evolutionary adaptation. It is why nature loves small errors.

So how can you learn to love small errors? The answer is in the question. Start small.

I've suggested you start with your relational behavior, and the foundation of good relationships is built upon good listening. So try starting there. Try implementing the model for balancing statement, question, and summary in, for example, your one-on-one meetings with your direct reports. Let them in on your plan by saying, "I'm trying something a little new in how I approach these meetings. At the end we'll talk about how it worked for both of us." If you're experimenting with relationships, it is essential you bring others into the process. By being open about a willingness to experiment and take chances, you encourage them to do the same.

In a workshop I taught, a senior executive was compelled by my invitation to take on a curious mindset in order to create psychological safety. He asked, "But how can we actually do it in practice?" My advice was simple: "Tell people what you're doing and why you're doing it, then do it. Like this: 'I'm practicing being more curious. That means I'll probably be asking more questions and listening more intently than I usually do. And I'm doing this to see if it helps to improve our collaboration style.'" Sharing your intentions out loud like this not only brings people into your process, it has the added benefit of holding you accountable to executing and learning from your experiment.

The scientific method usually begins with a hypothesis; the experiment that follows is a way to test that hypothesis. Don't be afraid to start with a hunch. Maybe you've noticed the more junior people in your team don't speak as much during meetings. Try a behavioral nudge to get the younger members to speak more while encouraging the more senior people to create space for deeper and wider (and safer!) participation. It may sound something like, "In our meeting today, I'd like to hear from everyone: a new insight, a question, or a response to someone else. And while we're at it, let's all assume positive intent so that we can make this happen."

Keep in mind that the scientific method isn't about one-off experiments. Repetition is essential if you want reliable results. Test. Calibrate. Repeat. Apply the same intervention in different environments, different scenarios. Gather data, which in your case will be qualitative: How are people responding? What does their body language tell you?

Direct and candid feedback is the ultimate data for a business leader, especially in this kind of work.* Open the door for greater candor in the feedback people give you by going deeper in your questions. After a presentation, instead of just asking, "How did I do?" ask, "What impact did my presentation have on you?"

Flip the script. Typically feedback flows only one way in one-on-one meetings with direct reports. Try soliciting "uphill" feedback from your direct reports, keeping in mind some may not initially feel comfortable doing so. Genuinely seeking constructive feedback from those who work for you can go a long way in creating a culture of continuous learning— where everyone is open to getting better and no one is fearful of making mistakes. Be specific with your request and your intention. "I know that I get stressed when we get close to deadlines, and instead of listening to you, I tend to interrogate you. I really want to stop that behavior. Would you be willing to share with me one thing I could do to help you feel more heard and valued in moments of high stress?"

And that is the point of these experiments: not to get it right, but to learn.

---

* Remember our distinction between technical and adaptive challenges in chapter 25.

37

MESSING UP

I used to "mess up" countless times a day.

I'd miss emails I should have responded to. I wouldn't always follow through on things I'm supposed to take care of like expense reports, scheduling meetings, or attaching a file to an email. I would interrupt people. I would stop listening or get distracted in the middle of an intense moment for a client. I have regretted not speaking up when something went wrong. I have let too much time pass without offering an apology. I have assumed aspects of people's identities, assumed gender pronouns, and worse, misgendered individuals, even when I knew better. I have become impatient and upset with my children for what later seems like no good reason at all. I have, in some of these situations, caused harm. And I have learned that I can't undo that harm I caused just by apologizing.

As hard as that was to write, I assume that these kinds of "mess ups" are familiar to you too, which makes it a bit easier for me to swallow. And perhaps my own admissions give you permission to be more forgiving of yourself. That forgiveness is essential and is the reason I say, "I *used to* mess up." I still make mistakes, of course. But I have shifted my perspective on messing up. Today, for example, I give myself more leniency and grace around my responsiveness to email. The pressure to respond quickly is,

I've learned, false. When I take the time I need to respond, I find that the worst-case scenario I'd dreamed up in my head was far removed from reality. People generally forgive, don't notice, or even appreciate the reality of a delayed response—because it gives them permission, implicitly, to take their time too. To slow down, think, and be thoughtful, instead of being reactive.

On the other hand, I count misgendering as a significant mess up, and a harmful one. When I have assumed a quality or experience of someone's identity and was wrong, I have caused harm. I count letting too much time pass thinking about it but without actually offering my apology an embarrassing, cringey, and disappointing mistake. Some of my failed attempts to repair have fractured relationships. I've learned the hard way, and I assume I'll continue to learn in this way.

We are going to mess up, big and small. We are going to do things that we wish we hadn't. We are going to make mistakes because we *don't* know better. And we are going to make mistakes even when we *do* know better. The cringe response is actually a good thing. Can you imagine if your mistake didn't make you feel bad, guilty, or embarrassed? We have a word for that: sociopath!

I'm not just talking about a failure to act. I'm talking about those times we behave in a way that is incongruent with who we mean to be, or how we perceive ourselves. How do we do that less often? How do we recover? How do we repair damage or hurt? Lucky for you, I can share some pointers—all of them learned the hard way!

First, **accept** that you will make mistakes, both when you know better and when you don't know better. Understand that mistakes serve a purpose: to teach you something new and to move you closer to the person and leader you see yourself to be.

Second, when you make a mistake, **acknowledge** what happened and why it might have happened. What assumptions or biases caused you to think or act in a way that turned out to be harmful? Explore the roots of those beliefs. Be careful not to attribute too much (or too little) blame to yourself. Try to be realistic and objective about what happened, but also acknowledge your feelings. Nothing will change if you don't honor your feelings.

To pull an example from my life, I once forgot to turn on the closed-captioning and subtitles during our video conference even though I knew there was at least one person who was hard of hearing on the call and who would have had a better experience if the closed-captioning was on. I'm embarrassed by my oversight; it's an easy thing to turn on the captions, and I wish I had remembered to do it. My root bias here is that most of the time in such talks, people don't need or ask for accommodations. Maybe I had a root belief that it's not my responsibility alone to offer and ensure accommodations. Maybe in a moment of forgetfulness, I was simply biased by the dominant culture's way of communicating, which has such a strong hold on us. We must reflect so that we can understand where the bias came from in the first place, and reduce the chances of it happening again.

This brings me to my third tip: take immediate action to **repair** any damage done by your mistake. In my real-world example, I told myself, "To ensure this does not happen again, I will turn on automatic subtitles by default on our video calls. I will reach out to all the participants to apologize for my oversight and will send them the written transcript of the call first thing in the morning."

You're not done there! To ensure that the learning actually sticks, it's helpful to **reflect** on how you felt after you repaired or apologized. The day after I sent the transcript of the call, I was able to acknowledge that it wasn't as bad as I thought it was going to be. The participants were appreciative; one even said she'd made the same mistake before and that my email helped her to see the power of courageously owning your mistakes. I was reminded that integrity and courage are leadership qualities I want to continue to nurture in myself.

Of course, those tips are helpful once harm is done. But it's also obviously helpful to *prevent* harm in the first place. By **building diverse relationships**, you're more likely to embrace inclusive practices. I'd like to think that if I had closer relationships with people who are deaf, I wouldn't have made this mistake, for example. **Do research on people's backgrounds** once you know what their avowed identities are. And make a habit of actively **seeking out diverse perspectives** so you can understand how your own view has been shaped.

Finally, in the spirit of the title of this book, I again encourage you to **continue experimenting**. Paradoxically, the more you experiment and the more risks you take, the smaller and more containable your errors will be (in general). Playing it safe sets us up for really disastrous mistakes. By normalizing risk, you will also be normalizing error and creating an environment in which it is easier to recover from error. You will create a culture of learning and growth.

To close, a note about apologizing. My favorite book on the topic is *Why Won't You Apologize?* by Harriet Lerner.[*] Apology can be a delicate experience; it's easy to under or over apologize. I have found that the best apology is an honest, short, and direct one, without too much fluff or drama. "I'm so sorry that I left off the captions. It was an oversight on

---

[*] Harriet Lerner, *Why Won't You Apologize? Healing Big Betrayals and Everyday Hurts* (UK: Gallery Books, 2017).

my part, and I'm committing to turning on automatic captions on all our video calls going forward and learning from my mistake." Avoid the temptation to overexplain—or worse, invite sympathy, which makes it about you. The point of the apology is to acknowledge, reflect, learn, and move on. And when you receive an apology, I've learned that the best response is simply "Thank you."

We must also acknowledge the essential corollary of apology, which is forgiveness. If we are to repair harm by apologizing as a first step, then we need to extend the same grace to others who are on their own imperfect leadership journeys and offer *them* forgiveness as a first step. Give people slack. Recognize that we all make mistakes and most of the time, our mistakes are unintentional. I've struggled to understand forgiveness for some time, but in a conversation I had with my coach about someone hurting me, I suddenly saw things clearly. She said that forgiveness sounds like this: "I may not accept what you did or even understand why you did it, but I am no longer going to punish you for it." I love this so much that I have started to share it with clients. It is a very powerful way to restore relationships and bring back a sense of justice.

PART IV

HOW INCLUSIVE LEADERS EMERGE AND EVOLVE

38

ENDINGS AND BEGINNINGS

My reference to your inclusive journey in the singular shouldn't lead you to believe that this journey is a single, discrete, unified entity. It is, of course, plural. There are journeys within journeys, each nested inside each other like Russian dolls. Think of a screenplay, which is typically constructed around three acts. But it may have as many as ninety scenes, each of them a story unto itself, with their own arc, their own rise and fall. Screenwriters also think in terms of sequences: larger arcs composed of three or five or even more scenes—not quite an act but more than a scene. And so it is with the narrative of your life and the narrative of your evolution as an inclusive leader.

At RoundTable we have a ritual called Capstone that illustrates this layering of multiple journeys. Typically an all-day event, it comes after a company—sometimes just select leaders, but often all of their employees—has gone through our JEDI© training series.

I intentionally describe Capstone as a ritual. Rituals are important moments that help us mark, process, and understand change. They are a kind of storytelling device. Think of high school or college graduations, both clearly demarcating an end *and* a beginning. Or coming-of-age rituals around the world, like the bar and bat mitzvah in the Jewish tradition and the "thread ceremony" in my own Hindu tradition, which demarcates the stage of life when a person dedicates themself to the pursuit of knowledge and being a good citizen.

As the dictionary definition of *capstone* suggests, it is a culmination, a kind of summation of lessons and insights garnered during the training and of how people now feel differently about themselves. But like every ending, Capstone is also a beginning. We like to frame the coexistence of ending and beginning with the ideas of William Bridges—aptly named because he devoted his life to helping individuals and organizations understand and navigate the often-difficult dynamics of change and transition. He broke the process down into three phases:

- *Endings*: Endings involve some kind of loss, and we have to figure out how to manage that loss. But as we figure out what to leave behind and let go of, and what we want to keep and carry on with us, we plant the seeds for a new beginning.

- *Neutral Zone*: It is neutral only in that it doesn't fully belong to the old reality we are leaving behind or to the new one we are stepping into. In many ways, it is the most active part of this process—our identity and thinking is realigning and finding new patterns.

- *New Beginnings*: When a new direction is clear, there is a great sense of energy and purpose. While we may have been disoriented in each of the previous two phases, now we have a clear compass and road map.*

During our Capstone ritual, we actually put Endings, Neutral Zone,

---

* William Bridges, *Managing Transitions: Making the Most of Change* (Reading, MA: Addison-Wesley, 1991).

and New Beginnings on three different walls, then ask participants to stand in the area they most identify with at that moment. It's both fascinating and revealing to see how differently the same change event can be experienced and internalized by a group of coworkers. Imagine the longtime CEO of your company was leaving. If you were close to them, this transition could feel very much like an ending. Another employee with a different relationship with the old CEO, or someone who had only recently been hired, might identify with one of the other phases.

We also have a Crossing the Line ritual that is almost always moving and powerful. First, we ask all our participants (some of whom have shied away from thinking of themselves as leaders) to *name* themselves as a leader. Then we ask them to take the first concrete steps toward *being* that leader. They name and share in specific terms the nature of their commitment. Sometimes in this naming experience, they articulate what kind of help or support they need from others or they acknowledge people who helped them get to this stage. It's a beautiful ritual that brings people together to share and hold each other accountable.

We then have them cross a line taped on the floor to actualize this commitment and transition. This simple step across a symbolic line involves multiple realizations: Who was I before? Who am I now? Who do I aspire to be? What am I leaving behind? What am I taking with me? As in the LEAD framework, by this point our leaders' identities are decided.

39

USING THE NEGATIVES

DISAPPOINTMENT

Our Capstone events, like any ritual, can be a powerful and moving experience for those who participate. This is especially the case when the JEDI© trainings have been largely or exclusively virtual. The work of inclusion can be intense and intimate. It demands vulnerability. It's understandable, therefore, that people would want to connect in person for a culminating Capstone session.

The Rolling Stones shared this hard truth in their song "You Can't Always Get What You Want." It sometimes takes people a while to fully understand that disappointment is, in fact, built into the ethos of inclusive work. Hearing everyone's voice and point of view actually increases the likelihood of disagreement and tension. Conflict and compromise are part of the messiness of inclusion.

Such was the case with a client who was planning on an in-person Capstone event but, because of COVID-19 concerns, moved the event to a fully virtual format at the last minute. Rather than encouraging people to get over their disappointment, my co-leader and I made it an explicit topic of discussion. And as Deep Democracy teaches us, in leaning into dissent and resistance, we found some gold. In the discussion, a useful distinction was made between *hearing* people—with empathy—and *satisfying* them. Asking for what you need isn't the same thing as getting it. Being heard, in fact, brings that disappointment out into the open while honoring and validating it. Inclusion and disappointment go hand in hand in this case. But because we are heard, the disappointment doesn't linger and fester.

NEVER-ENDING FEEDBACK

We can never please everyone. But the desire to please is real and understandable and surfaces time and time again in my work. One instance was in a conversation with a client about feedback. Healthy organizations thrive on good feedback. We've touched repeatedly on the importance of feedback to inclusive leadership.

This particular client was, on the one hand, a model in actively soliciting and being open to feedback from colleagues and direct reports. She wanted feedback and wanted to improve and be better. The problem was the feedback just kept coming. There was always something for her to improve on. It was as if she could never quite get it right, never fully please people.

This seemingly endless loop is intrinsic to any evolutionary process. Evolution is never finished, and neither is our personal or professional growth. And yet I understood and empathized with where she was coming from. In a RoundTable session, where we coach a small group of leaders together, I asked her to separate her feelings about her imperfect journey from the feedback she was getting from others. "Why give others the power to determine how you feel?" I asked her point-blank.

The point wasn't that she shouldn't have feelings. It was that how she emotionally processed her progress along her path should be her choice and hers alone. Feedback from others was just useful data for her to use as she saw fit.

Inclusive leadership thrives on good feedback. And it thrives on candor. Part of the emotional intelligence required of inclusive leaders is taking ownership of your own emotional state so that the tough feedback, candid opinions, dissent, and resistance you will inevitably field don't throw you off emotionally.

40

LOWERING THE WATERLINE

I've used this phrase throughout the book. It's more than just a different way to say "talking about the elephant in the room." Lowering the waterline can feel like an almost physical act; it's not just revealing previously unspoken things but releasing previously blocked energy. It's often dramatic and moving, acting as a catalyst for real change.

One such instance took place in a discussion about psychological safety at an investment firm. The term psychological safety evokes positives like trust and validation; but part of understanding what it means to feel safe is to tap into what it means to feel *unsafe*. To access that understanding, I might ask a variation of the following questions: What are the conditions that allow you to speak freely? What prevents you from freely sharing your ideas at work? Can you recall a time when you felt bad or ashamed for asking a question at work? It's good to get these questions out there, but more often than not, they don't prompt a lot of participation. People are reluctant to voice these feelings and experiences—*especially* if they involve the very organization or people they are currently working for. It takes a lot of courage to speak up. Yet when one person does, it unleashes other voices and a whole lot of bottled-up energy and emotion.

On this day, the discussion about feeling unsafe seemed to be heading down the typical path where people hold back. But then Amber, a respected veteran and senior partner, spoke up. She spoke frankly about what it was like being a pioneer at a firm (and in an industry) that for decades had very much been an "old boys' club." When she started in the '90s, there hadn't even been a women's bathroom. She had to go downstairs and to the nearby sandwich shop anytime she needed to use the bathroom. She paused to let that sink in. She went on to reveal she "wouldn't dare ask" to leave work early to take care of her kids, which frequently forced her into difficult and impossible choices.

Amber was the only woman at meetings, and time and time again, she would make a point, and it would be ignored. Then a man would make essentially the same point, and suddenly it registered and was taken up enthusiastically. She felt it almost didn't matter what she said. She talked about these and other instances almost matter-of-factly. "I was doing my time," she said, "so you all wouldn't have to go through the same thing." She'd articulated a message I hear all the time, especially from women of color. They don't focus on the difficulty of their own struggle; they look to see who's coming behind them.

She even called out people in the firm—though she didn't use names, it was still bold and powerful. "There are people in this very meeting who would prevent me from entering a room. Who would avoid inviting me to a happy-hour gathering. I fought my way to where I am today."

Though the story of women's marginalization in corporate boardrooms is familiar across America today, what Amber did that day was groundbreaking. There had never been a discussion like this at the firm. Much less a message like this coming from a senior partner. And on the first day of JEDI!©

The men on the call started to weigh in. "Amber, we had no idea—"

But Amber quickly clarified where she was coming from. "I'm not looking for an apology. I want you to know how things were. And how things were is not at all in the rearview mirror, even if the firm is now 50 percent women. Fighting for a seat at the table is one thing. But I know I still have to fight to *keep* that seat. And I know there are others who are still fighting to get there. That's who I'm speaking for."

Now, this meeting had clear gender dynamics, but there were other power dynamics at play as well. This was a CEO-less firm run by its senior partners, Amber among them. But also in the meeting were associates and interns. Asha, one of the associates, spoke up.

"Since we're being vulnerable and transparent," she said, "I feel I need to address the huge gap between the people who have all the power and influence, and who seem to matter, and those who have virtually no power and influence and who don't seem to matter as much."

It was another mic-drop moment. Here the firm was, on the first day of learning how to build a more inclusive culture. Yet they had their own long history of exclusion, which they had never properly reckoned with. That exclusion was still present, in various forms, and still wasn't being dealt with. It had been swept under the rug. But Amber and Asha had pulled that rug back.

To the firm's credit, they were up to the challenge. After this first two-year pilot of JEDI,© Amber immediately said they wanted to renew for another two years. After that second two years, one of the male senior partners (who incidentally had been both apologetic and defensive in that first session) approached me and said he'd love to go through it a third time but wanted to give others the opportunity. He had found the program so valuable and still wanted ongoing maintenance and guidance on how to take these principles and apply them in daily practice. Out of that discussion came a whole new offering at RoundTable we call Inclusive Leadership Labs (ILL), where we turn the JEDI© learnings into real applications for the particular company. This senior partner, four years later, continues to attend the ILLs and share his journey and, importantly, the lessons he has learned along the way and the new commitments he's making to be a kinder and more inclusive leader. People who attend the ILLs along with him are moved by his vulnerability, and he reminds them all the time that he was influenced by Amber's words years ago in that first JEDI© session.

All because one woman dared to lower the waterline.

SCROLLING BUBBLES

Lowering the waterline played out very differently, in a more collective way, in another session, one for high-potential women leaders in a large media company. With about sixty-five women on the call, I had only an hour to introduce them to inclusive leadership, so I had to use my time wisely and cover only the most critical elements. As I've made clear, I believe a lot of progress can be made just by focusing on improving our listening skills. So I decided to do a primer on listening in the Me channel and in the You channel.

As we've covered previously, listening in the Me channel is much more than a focus on how something affects or resonates with you. It's also about learning to listen to your own inner voice. You can't be an effective leader and advocate until you are in tune with (and then can later hone and leverage) that voice.

We use a tool that allows participants to write down what they hear their inner voice saying, in an almost stream-of-consciousness way. Anonymously, those messages appear on a shared screen in "scrolling bubbles." It's a powerful way to bring the unsaid and unspoken out into the open while maintaining safety and allowing people to remain anonymous.

On this day, after a discussion on the different types of listening I asked the participants to share what kinds of messages they hear from their inner voice regularly and write them in the tool. After an anticipatory pause, messages like the following started appearing on the screen:

I'm not smart enough to be in this group.

I'm too old to be a leader.

I don't understand what is going on most of the time.

I've never been thin enough and will never reach my ideal weight.

Nobody believes me when I talk.

They don't want me in the inner circle.

I'll never get a seat at the table.

I'm not allowed to make mistakes.

I don't belong here.

I have to change myself too much to fit in.

My accent is too thick and people don't understand me.

I allowed the messages to scroll down uninterrupted and didn't say anything. One after another, these painful messages scrolled across the shared screen, collectively portraying the inner dialogue of these high-potential woman. There were so many messages, all ringing of this same quality: I'm not enough, and I don't belong.

Eventually, one courageous woman took herself off mute and turned her video on. "I see myself in those words," she shared gently, sadly. "I don't know if this is a good thing or a bad thing, but I just don't feel alone anymore."

Another woman joined in. "It's good to know I'm not the only one with these feelings."

And yet another. "I never felt safe saying how I felt, but if so many of us feel this way, it seems we should be able to express it."

We had lowered the waterline on what one had permission to say in the group. Through their tears, the women saw that in their feelings of aloneness and vulnerability, they could be seen and understood. This was only possible when they were allowed to be anonymous—when they could hide, essentially. But the common ground of their emotion gave them the courage to stop hiding and share publicly. Emotion is often the bridge to inclusion because it is a universal language. What they saw was that one voice was all voices.

So yes, in this case, lowering the waterline also resulted in releasing the waterworks. That is not uncommon when people suddenly feel truly understood. My closest friends tease that I can make people cry with just a look or a smile, which isn't entirely true . . . it's more than just me and my coaching style. There's a larger dynamic at work here. Lowering the waterline exposes hidden and suppressed emotions, and those often get expressed through tears.

I am frankly quite fascinated by tears. They can express sadness or joy, or both at once. Often, they represent an emotion that doesn't have a word in English: a kind of freedom, an experience of being seen by others or even by oneself in a new way for the first time.

Known for my direct questions, I do often ask clients, "What do those tears mean for you?" To others, I may ask, "What's it like to see so-and-so crying?" And yes, that sometimes brings even more tears. But it also brings clarity to the experience of being seen and understood. These questions lower the waterline by giving people permission to feel, be themselves, and belong.

On this day, my clients seemed to understand that, even though their tears grew out of painful experiences of *not* belonging, of *not* feeling safe, their tears in this moment were about connection, belonging, and inclusion. I wanted to harness the power of the moment and the shared power the women were feeling. I continued the exercise of Me-channel listening and asked them to write down, on a new screen, what they would say to themselves the next time they heard their inner voice telling them they were not good enough or that they did not belong. This time, the bubbles started appearing more quickly.

You go, girl!

You are enough.

You belong.

You are here for a reason.

You can make a difference.

All your hard work has led you to this moment. You deserve this.

Rest. You're worth it.

I love you.

You are a leader.

The scrolling bubbles felt like a celebration. "I feel powerful just reading these!" one woman said through her tears.

Another said, "Imagine if we all felt like this all the time—there would be no stopping us!"

Powerfully, one person said, "Imagine our daughters and sons are feeling unsure of themselves all the time. We could be the voice for change for them, and by speaking these words to them, we get to hear them too."

The contrast was stark: the women viscerally experienced the shift from feeling despondent to powerful in mere moments, just by using their listening and their voice in a new way. Their new battle cry was grounded in a sense of togetherness. They emerged feeling less alone in the journey to self-actualization. Though it is, in fact, a lonely journey, when we are reminded that we are all on the journey, albeit at different points, it helps us and moves us forward. These women were only reminded of that fact, though, because we safely lowered the waterline to uncover what was swimming beneath.

41

THE IMPORTANCE OF DANCING

FIRST, DISARM

There is an ancient Irish saying: "You don't give a man a weapon until you've taught him how to dance." The idea is that, before someone can responsibly wield power or an actual physical weapon, they have to undergo the kind of inner work that art (among other things) makes possible. Michael Meade, a writer who specializes in myth, explores this idea in his podcast episode "The March of Violence." When we express ourselves artistically, Meade says, we are prompted to "know the wounds" of our souls.* If someone wields power without going through this inner journey, they will likely be unmoved by the suffering of others and apt to project their unexamined wounds onto others.

The heart of the matter, Meade says, is that "in order to properly bear arms, a person must first become disarmed." I love this idea that a person should lay down their defenses before thinking of wielding power or a weapon. That dance is chosen as the metaphor for self-expression and

---

* Michael Meade, "The March of Violence," episode 135, *Mosaic Voices*, podcast.

251

vulnerability makes me love it even more. It's part of the reason, despite some publishers' feedback, that I started this book with my own disarming, my own dance. There are, of course, many ways to be vulnerable. But with dance, you have nothing but your soul and your body, and you put both on the line. There's a unique kind of exposure involved. Perhaps that's why the coaching mantra of "dancing in the moment" has resonated so much with me over the years.

Vulnerability and authenticity are good practices for everyone in the workplace (and in life). But the old Irish saying really does drive home why this is especially critical for people with privilege and power. Even without a physical weapon, you do have the power to wound. We've all seen leaders unwittingly do so.

Indeed, some of the most moving and transformative moments in my work have been exactly those times when someone in power, especially a CEO, chose to be vulnerable. You don't want to dance with someone who's armed. But when someone in power voluntarily lays down their arms, suddenly so much seems possible.

DANCING WITH DEFENSIVENESS

There are two kinds of techniques in the martial arts, hard and soft, and each martial arts style is largely associated with one or the other. In the hard school (karate and tae kwon do are prime examples), the objective is to meet force with force; the underlying disposition is to be unyielding. In the soft school (epitomized by judo, jujitsu, and aikido), yielding is, in fact, the objective. The strategy is to absorb the opponent's force and energy, go with it, move with it, and then end up using that very force against them.

The principle of *ju* is at the heart of all of the soft martial arts and can be translated as *soft* or *yielding*. Kano Jigoro, the founder of judo, believed fundamentally in the principle of "softness overcoming hardness." A key technique in any move is *kuzushi*, or *unbalancing*.

There's a bit of this dynamic in how I approach dancing in the moment—particularly when that moment features defensiveness, resistance, or even passive-aggressiveness on the part of the person or group I am working with. Only my objective isn't to defeat an opponent or unbalance them to throw them off. It is to break stasis and deadlock, to get us unstuck. Instead of throwing my client to the floor, I want us both up and moving and dancing.*

If this sounds a little esoteric, let me illustrate with a story. Back when I was working for LightHouse, I had a male client, Victor, who had a reputation for being difficult to coach. And of course, they paired him with me! I had a reputation for savoring the challenge of supposedly impossible-to-coach types.

In our very first session, he laid his cards out on the table. "I haven't had good experiences working with women. And I definitely don't like working with psychologists. But you are both of those things, and I know I have to be here." He was telling me I already had two strikes against me; he'd just infused power and force into our dynamic, in a very unbalanced way.

I could have been defensive in return. Perhaps in another setting I

---

* As a side note, although judo is a competitive sport and the objective is to win, empathy and consideration are seen as core values and, in a sense, are more important than the outcome. The bow before and after any competition—critically, with eye contact—is all about recognition.

253

might have been. But a coaching relationship gives us permission to set aside those default reactions, to sit with difficulty and discomfort, and to experiment with ways of working through it.

I wasn't thinking about martial arts at the moment, but my response was classic judo. I yielded. "Actually, you *don't* have to be here."

Victor was surprised and a little thrown off. I continued. I chose to focus not on the substance of his words—which could have been taken as sexist and preemptively passive-aggressive—but on the intent behind them.

"It sounds like you don't *want* to be here." I probed further, but gently. I wanted to know *for his sake* what experiences might have prompted these feelings. I asked what was behind his declaration about not wanting to work with women or psychologists.

In that moment, the energy shifted. I think he could tell that my questions weren't a tactic.

It turns out he'd had a bad experience with couples counseling, which in one stroke had soured him on the idea of working with women and psychologists. It wasn't exactly a revelation (not yet), but his willingness to share and open up got us moving together. Later, in a group coaching session, the revelation did come. Entirely on his own initiative, Victor brought up the rocky start to our coaching relationship. He said he believed in equity for women and realized they had historically been at a disadvantage and that something needed to be done about that. But in all of these conversations about inclusion, he said, there was no recognition of the challenge and reality of being a man in this time of change. His resistance to me, to women in general, was catalyzed by his own marginalization, which was complex and layered.

This wasn't a case of male grievance. Victor was extremely heartfelt and vulnerable, in a way none of us had ever seen before. He softened, his eyes and cheeks tender and pink. The group (many of whom were women) responded in kind, with empathy. He confessed that he had never had a sense of being heard in the way he felt he was then. I and the other women could certainly relate. In this moment of openness, we had that shared experience in common, even as we were coming from different levels of privilege. It was a reminder of the fact that inclusion isn't just about making room for those who historically have been excluded (although that's certainly a defining goal). It's about hearing the voices and recognizing the lived experience of everyone. Everyone.

It was a breakthrough moment for this particular client. When Victor had the chance to renew our coaching contract after six months, he did. Four years later, he was at another company and I had started Round-Table. He reached out to me and shared, "Priya! I just got promoted to partner! I look back and can't believe I put all those obstacles in my own way. And all I kept remembering was that group coaching session that helped me clear my path. I get it, finally. Thank you." He was all in.

This (and many other similar experiences) have taught me never to dismiss the potential of any one individual to evolve into an inclusive leader. Sometimes, the energy behind their initial resistance is exactly what fuels their later growth.

42

"I'M NOT READY"

"We are not going to talk today about diversity," a CEO, who in many ways was deeply committed to the mission of inclusion, said to me as we were planning a RoundTable session. Clients may have many reasons to express hesitancy about wading into difficult and sometimes uncomfortable topics. Often they are feeling the pressure of business imperatives and worry that difficult conversations will sidetrack the team. In these moments, they want to (whether they explicitly articulate this or not) step back and put their inclusion efforts on autopilot or a lower gear or on the back burner. A different reason emerged in this case.

I didn't fight the CEO in our one-on-one meeting. But as the group session started, it was clear to me that diversity was exactly what we were going to talk about. The team had been skirting around the issue, saying things like, "*Some people* don't understand . . ." and, "I don't want to *name names* but . . ." and, "We have *certain dynamics* here that create challenges."

As a facilitator, I have to share what I'm noticing, with equanimity, and give the system an opportunity to respond and decide where to take it. My belief is that others notice, or will notice, the same things too, they're just not naming them. "What I'm sensing," I told them, "is that things like race, gender, and bias are the elephants in the room. I also know that we are here because you want to evolve as a culture. What do you want to do?"

The CEO gave me a look, but we had a strong rapport and trust and we both felt fortified by it. I wasn't doing it to be contrarian for the sake of it. I just find that lowering the waterline is almost always the way to go. I share my voice in this way to model the practice of sharing my truth and also to open up the ground to multiple truths in the room. Sharing those truths moves the group to new heights.

We had a long, emotional discussion about why these topics were so difficult to discuss. Eventually the CEO spoke. "We're not ready," he stated flatly. Then he thought it over and corrected himself. "*I'm* not ready," he said with a shaky voice and tears in his eyes.

It was a powerful moment. This was one of my client's greatest strengths: his willingness to model vulnerability, to be candid about what he was feeling in the moment. That is the raw material I need to work with as a coach. It ended up being a great session. Why? Because multiple truths were shared and the group learned that nobody has a monopoly on the truth—an unexpected but compelling lesson. But the session, to be frank, was not a sustainably transformative one. The company continued on a stop-and-start pattern I see not infrequently with clients, where inclusion is a high priority for some stretches but not so much at other times.

Still, the leadership team learned something new about truth and about courage. So often, behind the defensiveness, deflections, or rationalizations of an individual leader or an entire team is the simple fact that they don't feel ready. To that I counter with two observations. First, you never feel fully ready—or, when you do, the feeling doesn't last long when you come up against just how tough the work is. Second, that "not ready" feeling is a form of resistance, which is a sign that now is precisely the time to go deeper. Pushing against that friction will invariably generate heat and wisdom and insight.

43

"I'M STILL THE SAME GUY"

This brings to mind another supposedly impossible-to-coach story. This client was with a private equity firm that invested heavily in biotech. Getting the science right was, obviously, integral to their business, but so were people skills. The firm's long-term objective was not just to invest in start-ups but to groom their own people to take a leadership role in those companies.

Hank had no interest in the leadership part of the equation. He was all about the science. And his laser focus on the science led to frequent bursts of angry impatience with colleagues who he felt hadn't done their homework. He had a reputation as an asshole and, in fact, proudly declared so in our first coaching session. He wore it as a badge of honor.

I did two things in that first session that taught both Hank and me something important. First, as I'd done with Victor, I didn't call him out on his rudeness. Instead, I recalled that one of my core principles of inclusion is that everyone gets to define themselves as they wish. Hank's defining himself as an asshole was curious to me, and it was meaningful to him. With Hank, I focused on intent. "What is your goal?" I asked him. "What are you trying to accomplish with these outbursts?" Then, going with rather than against his fundamental scientific mindset, I asked him to look at the data. "Do your outbursts seem to be working? Are you getting people to come to meetings better prepared?"

Hank had to confess that, no, his current strategy didn't appear to work. Though it gave him a confidence boost, it didn't seem to shift the team dynamics for the better.

"I'm not an empathetic person, Priya." There's that definition of self again.

I was Socratic in my approach. "What does it mean to be empathetic?" I inquired.

To his credit, he admitted that he didn't know. So he took it up as a kind of scientific project. He read deeply about empathy and emotional intelligence. He soon found out that reading about empathy was very different from *being* empathetic. But he kept at it and put himself under a microscope. He made tweaks in his approach, noted the results, and reported them to me. In his own way, he went 100 percent with what I recommend to leaders all the time: experiment with your behavior in the real-life laboratory of your daily interactions, observe the data, adjust as necessary.

Hank was relentless. After our first six-month contract was over, he chose to renew (one of only two out of a cohort of nineteen to do so, which is a real testament to Hank's commitment to growing). Slowly but surely, he remade himself (or at least his behavior), and his reputation shifted. He opened himself up to the idea of taking a leadership role in a start-up. For my part, I learned just how important it is to accept people's definitions of themselves and leverage them for change. Though we might disagree with people's definitions of themselves, instead of denying their self-defined identity ("You're not an asshole, Hank!"), we must remain curious about where their definitions come from. It is up to each of us to define ourselves as we wish, iterate those definitions, and share them with others. Hank identified as a scientist, an asshole, and not empathetic—to start. So we used those definitions of himself to get him to a new place.

When a leadership role at a new company opened up and Hank was selected, he took the position, but he also knew this was a test. Thinking like a scientist, he realized that, with his new colleagues, he would be starting with a blank slate. Their assessment of him as a leader would be a clear and objective measure of just how far he'd come. Again, very much to his credit, he was truly curious (and you know how much I like curiosity!). Would he be seen as an empathetic leader? "Let's see what happens," he told me.

When the first round of reviews from his direct reports came in, the overwhelming consensus was that Hank was an incredibly warm and empathetic leader, but he didn't stop there. He reached out to me to bring JEDI© training to his new company. I hadn't seen him for a while, and he approached me to say, "Remember me? I'm still an asshole. I'm still the same guy."

Was he? I don't know, and it's not for me to say. But Hank's remarkable transformation as a leader—and the way he chose to frame it—tells us some important things. It's meaningful that Hank gets to define himself as he wishes to, and it's important that the texture and experience of that identity can shift and develop into something new and beautiful.

Ideally, the heart—emotional intelligence and empathy—will work in tandem with the head—tweaking your behavior and observing like a scientist. But that balance will be different for everyone. Some might be inclined to start from the heart and then work inside-out to alter their behavior. Some might take a more technical, outside-in approach, tinkering with their behavior in a more scientific way. Neither is better than the other, and great inclusive leaders will allow for varying styles of personal and professional growth.

I've said repeatedly that great leaders know their own stories—really well. But we all tell our own stories through a different lens. We get to choose how we name and craft our narrative. For Hank, it seemed to be important for him to say he was still the same guy. In the previous story, Victor most decidedly did *not* want to be what he called "that guy"—the man who gets in the way of greater inclusion for women. He wanted to change and was emotional and vulnerable through that process. Hank was more clinical and removed.

There is tremendous diversity in our journeys and in the stories we tell about them.

44

"MY BOSS IS CRAZY"

At one point, I conducted a JEDI© training for a professional association, a group of people who didn't actually work with one another on a daily basis. With this kind of dynamic, it can be a little harder to get people to open up because they don't know each other. We were in our third session, and the discussion was focused on managing microaggressions. We discussed a case study where a Black employee confessed to his boss that, in the wake of Breonna Taylor's murder, he was disappointed to the point of despair that the company had failed to step forward and issue a strong statement. In this scenario, the boss sent extremely mixed messages. He said this really wasn't a work-related issue. On the other hand, he said he wanted to be there for the employee. Yet on the *other* other hand, he came back to the fact that the employee had been distracted and unfocused on the job. The microaggression here was a kind of performative empathy paired with actual dismissal.

One of the participants chimed in and shared they'd had similar problems with their boss. They added, as an aside, "My boss is so crazy." That in turn sparked a side conversation of stories about "crazy" bosses. Now I think there were a few things going on here. For a group of people who don't know one another well, trading stories about being unhappy with the boss is low-hanging fruit. It can be a way to share in a common experience; the expressions were authentic and created intimacy. But the language deployed was sloppy. The boss in the case study wasn't crazy; he was insensitive.

We were about to move on to the next slide when a woman who hadn't spoken up asked if we could pause. The discussion had troubled her. She'd had a husband with dementia, and people had sometimes described him as acting crazy, which he wasn't. The woman, rightly, wasn't comfortable with the group throwing around an outdated term for talking about mental health in a conversation that had nothing to do with mental health. It muddied the issue and reinforced dangerous stereotypes about people struggling with mental health. It was its own kind of microaggression.

But that wasn't all. The woman also said she felt the term was much more likely to be used to describe women—as if women intrinsically weren't as in command of their faculties. She asked the first man who'd spoken up if his boss was a man or a woman. It was a woman. As we unpacked this issue, the group came to recognize just how gendered our use of the word *crazy* tends to be.

So, while discussing one microaggression, the group inadvertently stepped into another series of microaggressions, feeding into old stereotypes about both gender and mental health. The episode was a reminder of just how layered and multiple identity is. While we are talking about race, for example, gender dynamics do not magically disappear, even if we aren't paying close attention to them.

It is also a reminder of how very human and imperfect our inclusive journey is. We can feel we are making great progress in one area only to realize we have stalled in another. This story is of course about more than the notion that people stumble upon microaggressions in layered ways. To me, what's special is that people stayed with each other. The woman who spoke up did so with courage, not knowing what the outcome would be. And the people who listened to her also listened courageously, willing to be influenced by her, willing to have their minds changed. That is not failure or weakness but, rather, a sign of progress.

4 5

STANDING IN THE FIRE

In the stories in this final section of the book, I have tried to center my clients' experiences as they have learned to step up and evolve into stronger and more inclusive leaders. Inclusive work is very much a dialectic; it requires a complementary, synergistic energy between two or more people. In plainer language, it takes two (and often more) to tango. We need another person's energy to play off of, and when it's not there, our efforts can fall flat.

Coaching is successful when my client *and* I engage in great risk-taking and vulnerability. Of course, the relationship needs to withstand those risks; we must be courageous and offer each other safety, which I find comes from deeper intimacy and connection. I have found out the hard way that I cannot expect these qualities from them unless I am fully ready for whatever they might bring to the table that day: their confusion, their messiness, their resistance, their defensiveness. If I am not ready, if I have not cultivated a certain quality of equanimity, I can't expect from them the growth and learning I want to see, the growth and learning the world needs.*

---

* I will discuss the quality of equanimity at length in the conclusion.

267

This lesson was really driven home for me in a session with a leadership team from a financial-services and hedge-fund firm. The head of HR who had arranged the session gave me a warning ahead of time. "These aren't just conservative Republicans," she said, "but the kind who might be January sixth sympathizers." This made my heart race. That day in 2021 was the day that a mob of protestors attacked the United States Capitol and caused havoc across America. I felt uneasy and, frankly, scared. But I felt supported by HR and wanted to see how far we could go in service of learning and growth without tapping out.

"Maybe they are exactly the people who need this training the most," I said. Not knowing how receptive the company culture would be to full JEDI© training, we had put together a kind of introductory pilot workshop. We gave it the innocuous name Meaningful Conversations. It would likely be a tough crowd, she again emphasized, but she had hand-selected ten executives (all of whom turned out to be middle-aged white men) she felt had at least some desire to learn.

After several conversations with them individually where I sought to build rapport, trust, and safety, I was ready—or thought I was. For the first half of the three-hour session, I mostly got crickets. This kind of introductory workshop is designed to be participatory, but I got perfunctory responses at best. As I tend to do in most challenging situations, I leaned heavily into my "note and name" strategy. I noted the lack of feedback and participation and openly wondered what that might mean. Offering some vulnerability, I also noted that working with an unresponsive group caused me to worry about what was going wrong with the workshop and made me feel a little insecure. I emphasized that this slight insecurity was overridden by a desire to serve the group and provide some useful insights, so I was going to press on with that in mind. Often an overture of self-disclosure will inspire someone in the group to open up more in turn.

But this time, I still received almost nothing from the men in the room.

We closed with an exercise I call Paddles of Power. You imagine yourself on one side of a lake. Your objective is to get to the other side, and it's not going to be an easy crossing. The more paddles you have, the faster and easier the crossing will be. We go through a checklist of various forms of privilege, some obvious (like being white or male), others less so ("If you are in a body you would describe as fit, give yourself a paddle."). It's essentially a thought exercise in coming to terms with the many varieties of tailwinds and headwinds that come with privilege or the lack thereof. I emphasized that having more paddles (or tailwinds) doesn't mean you don't have to work and that your accomplishments are unearned, but your privilege *is* unearned.

The concrete nature of this thought exercise makes the advantages that come with privilege palpable to people in a new way. Participants often express an impulse to share some of their paddles with someone who has fewer. Not this group. For the first time all day, they spoke up, forcefully and defensively. "Are you saying I didn't work hard because I have all these paddles? Are you implying I'm inherently racist?"

I didn't exactly lose my cool, but I was definitely "hooked" by their commentary.[*] I was in a room with a group of angry white men who were turning their dissatisfaction with this exercise on me and doing so in a very personal way. I felt under attack. As I will explain in more depth later, equanimity starts with physical composure. Our brains don't distinguish a social threat from a physical attack. Unless we are really prepared, we tense up and our body cues us to be defensive. Instead of remaining open

---

[*] I use the term *hooked* in the same way one might use the word *triggered* to show that I was activated but not necessarily in a positive way. I am loath to use gun-related terminology to discuss facilitation given the politicization and proliferation of guns in America, against which I have something of a personal vendetta.

and curious, I defended the worth of the exercise. As we closed, I tried to salvage the day by saying that the group had raised valid questions, and I would address them later off-line.

———

The pilot had not been a success, at least according to my definition of success at that time. That became even clearer as the feedback came in. One participant said I had accused him of being a white supremacist. I knew I had missed an opportunity, and I was genuinely upset about how the workshop had gone. Yet I was firm in my resolve. I sat down with the head of HR and said I wanted to meet with that exact same group again. I wanted to revisit all of the issues and objections they had raised and go deeper. I hadn't been prepared the first time, and I naively thought that the law of vulnerability—in that it creates connection and change—would save me. The next time I would be better prepared.

It's worth noting that even as part of our job as facilitators is to create safety, that very safety we create is precarious. We, too, as facilitators, can feel unsafe. We can feel threatened and put in a very vulnerable position. We must make hard decisions: Do we show our vulnerability and courage, or do we cower or push back? Do we get hurt or martyr ourselves?

I can't say that my decision to explain and justify the exercise was well-thought-out; I did what my intuition dictated to me after years of practice. When there is "fire" in the system, as there was that day with the hedge-fund managers, our instincts kick in rather than careful, deliberate thought. Fire is urgent and fierce, and it comes unexpectedly. Part of a facilitator's preparation is knowing how they are likely to react to the fire. So while I was upset with the outcome at the time, looking back, I have to give myself grace that my defensiveness was vulnerable. It was an attempt to preserve safety for the group and very much for myself.

We scheduled a second session, but I didn't exactly get a do-over—or even a chance at round two. A few of the same men were there, but it was largely a different group altogether. The three who had led the counter-attack on me were absent. It was a more diverse group with two Indian women and one Black man. That diversity certainly made a difference. The all-white, all-male makeup of the first group encouraged a kind of tribalism. Conversely, the presence of women and people of color was, for the white men in the group, a bit of a check on their privilege, prompting them to see things through the lens of a lived experience not their own and to at the very least think before lashing out at me. But even aside from the composition of the group (the effect of which I do think was significant), the men who had been present the first time were completely different the second time around. They were receptive and engaged in the material in a thoughtful and meaningful way.

I think it's worth considering a couple of other factors that made the second session more productive. First, I began with a mea culpa—I acknowledged that I had messed up and had allowed myself to get defensive. I also shared with them that I *wished* I had remained open, curious, and nimble; asked questions, listened, and learned; and found clarity. In opening on that note, I modeled the skills of a good inclusive leader—specifically the practice of repair. You acknowledge messing up, but you don't linger over it; you try to learn from the experience and share that learning with others so you can all be better.

Second, I think there is a great deal of power in the act of standing in the fire with people in an uncomfortable or even adversarial situation.*

---

* For more on this idea, see Larry Dressler's 2010 book *Standing in the Fire: Leading High-Heat Meetings with Clarity, Calm, and Courage.*

However imperfectly, I had stood in the fire with the first group. I didn't lose my cool, I remained engaged and willing to listen, and I made it clear that the listening and learning would continue and that I wasn't done with them. Even had the same group returned intact, I think the results would have been different. I have seen this play out again and again with clients both in groups and in one-on-one sessions. When we experience a rough patch, I stay with them; I make it clear I'm not going anywhere and I want to see this through. I insist on connection and reciprocal learning. That persistence pays off. Sometimes, the initial resistance or opposition to inclusive teaching is a kind of test: they're almost daring you to dismiss them. When you don't, you will have earned their respect and a degree of openness.

These hedge-fund managers taught me some important lessons. I knew I had to examine my own biases around what it means to be ready. I thought I had the tools, but I was taught otherwise. I could see, crystal clear, just what *not* being ready could cost me in a challenging situation. I learned that readiness—which for me meant cultivating this quality of equanimity—was an essential aspect of allyship.

So my individual resolve was solidified along with my larger resolve around the mission of RoundTable and about the journey of inclusive leadership my team and I had to go on. I've never again had a session as actively antagonistic as that first one. But these men were not outliers. People like that are in influential positions throughout society and throughout corporate America, making big decisions. I had to be ready, we had to be ready, to engage them.

I posted about the experience on social media and got a lot of response.

"These guys should be your fuel," someone said. And they were. The JEDI© program—at that point still in its infancy and not yet established as a featured offering—moved front and center. The whole experience was a wake-up call. This work is going to be meaningful. And it's going to be hard. But I knew I was ready to stand in the fire.

46

CHANGE STARTS (AND STOPS) AT THE TOP

In the best of all possible worlds, the impulse for change comes from the top down *and* from the bottom up. A CEO will be deeply committed to the work of inclusion and just as deeply engaged in the process. Other leaders will be similarly committed and bring their own ideas and initiative to the table. And rank-and-file employees will know they have support from top leadership and will be willing to take chances and step forward as leaders themselves.

Everyone plays a critical role in this process. Yet it does, as the cliché goes, start at the top. To some extent, that is a function of my own role. My initial conversations are with a CEO, who in the end has to make the final call as to whether or not to engage RoundTable's services. That illustrates the larger point: sustainable, meaningful, long-term change requires institutional support—the commitment of resources and systems. The CEO has to hire a head of inclusion and give them the resources and authority to do the job. They need to form a DEI steering committee and give them the necessary resources. They need to hire a company like RoundTable that knows how to guide companies through those important conversations and decisions. They need to invest in reviewing and overhauling hiring, recruitment, and promotion processes and procedures. The list goes on and on.

And yet, as important as the initiative and engagement of the CEO is and as much as I believe in the power of one, one person, regardless of title, is still just one person. Their influence is large but not unlimited. They operate under very real constraints, some out of their control.

As one case in point, I'll briefly share the story of a CEO who approached me when his company was still a start-up. It's not at all unusual for a CEO to seek coaching for themselves, but it is highly unusual in my experience for a CEO of a start-up to invest in its culture, and everyone at the company, at that very early stage. What made this client even more of an outlier is that the company operated in a very conservative space, one even more dominated by white men than is usually the case. But Yacob was determined to go against the grain of the industry and make inclusion a cornerstone of the company's culture. And with the two of us working closely together, the company made real headway in its early days in establishing a culture of trust and psychological safety. Employees commented that they were receiving more lucrative offers elsewhere but they were choosing to stay because of the culture.

But one of the constraints a start-up faces is the need for multiple rounds of funding. It's not like an angel investor comes along, writes a blank check, and then leaves you to run with it. It can take years to establish profitability. And investors usually want a share of the company and a say in how it is run.

The world of private equity in the United States has very little diversity, at least at the time of this writing. It is largely white, middle-aged, and male. And the pull that world has on a young start-up can be significant, not just in terms of formal decision-making but in terms of the informal means by which culture is created. We all know the stereotypical scenario of deals coming together over a round of golf. That is very real. Investors bond informally with entrepreneurs over the activities they like to pursue in their leisure time. And for certain wealthy white men, that means golf and sailing and whiskey and cigars.

Such activities are not my thing, and while there are of course exceptions, these social spheres do not have much representation from minorities, women, LGBTQIA+ people, or people of color. Without even thinking about it consciously, an investor will exclude someone like me from a round of golf or a round of drinks. They don't even think of it as an act of exclusion; it just wouldn't occur to them to invite me.

We've covered Amy Edmondson's early research on psychological safety, which shows trust and cohesion are reflected and built through a group's informal and unstated norms. When it becomes an unstated norm that some people get invited to a skiing trip with a certain investor and others don't, the message is clear: some people belong more than others. When that happens, no matter how deliberate and genuine your more formal initiatives around culture-building are, you will start to lose people. That happened with this young and promising start-up. The pull of the industry they operated in and the pull of the private equity that financed them was at times stronger than the founder's very real commitment to building a culture of trust, safety, and inclusion.

But Yacob had learned some very solid tools to have important, if hard, conversations. He'd use our coaching sessions to practice role-playing those essential conversations. He was a values-driven leader and didn't want to cave under the pressure of the private-equity firm to compromise on his values. Emboldened by a sense of righteousness, he strongly communicated with the leaders of the private-equity firm—over a good old-fashioned bourbon in Louisville, KY—that his vision for inclusion paved a clear line to better business results. "It took some persuading, and I'm not sure they are 100 percent convinced, but I'm fine with them being 50 percent convinced at this stage," he later shared with me. He had the security of a solid relationship with them, he had the situational awareness and malleability to take on the old boys' club persona, and he had the gusto to speak his truth. That moment proved important to their company.

Over time, though, the cards would show that 50 percent conviction wasn't always enough; nor was he alone enough to influence this very powerful group of men. Over the ensuing years, Yacob and the PE firm wrestled with the tension between serving justice and achieving bottom-line results. Ultimately, only when the company showed tremendous and sustainable financial growth did the PE firm come around to the idea that inclusion may have had something to do with it.

47

WHEN LISTENING CREATES THE AGENDA

In chapter 11 I told you about a formative stretch in the evolution of my coaching where, with the help of a willing coconspirator, I experimented with going entirely off script in a session. It was a thrilling high-wire act and produced good results. But not every session is always the right time and place to do so. Agendas have their purpose.

The tech start-up I told you about in the previous chapter provided me with the perfect opportunity to keep experimenting. Typically, it's only after a company becomes established that they realize culture is something that needs to be deliberately shaped and tended to. But in this case, Yacob felt strongly about making inclusion and a healthy culture a priority from day one. So I had the opportunity to be in on the ground floor. Because the company's culture was only just emerging, I began to view it as a laboratory. I paid attention to my own sense of comfort and risk. One day, when I found myself feeling a bit too comfortable with the groove we had settled into, I decided to shake things up.

Four months into the leadership team's developmental training, I made the decision to go into the full-day session without an agenda. At first, I wondered, *How are we going to fill the whole day?*

My opening check-in question is always important—never more so than on a day like this. It is not just an icebreaker but a way to generate real material, to see what's truly on their minds, to get people to make impromptu observations, to get them to go off script. That day, the question was: "What are you looking forward to in today's session? And what are you *not* looking forward to?"

The question is not a deliberate provocation. But its binary nature inevitably elicits contrasting responses. That leads to polarity, which leads to tension—which is almost always good for me as a coach. It's great raw material. Why is the very thing one person is looking forward to the thing someone else is not looking forward to?

Without going into the details of all that happened that day, we ended up having a great session, with more than enough material to fill our time. By starting out with polarity, we set the tone for polarity to be available to us in that space; it emerged again and again, giving us opportunities each time to lower the waterline and discover hidden biases, assumptions, and needs. I have mentioned that leaders need to make an effort to consistently check in with themselves to notice how they are feeling, what is comfortable, and what feels risky. Leaders also need to pay attention to the actual nature of their attention, what psychologists call "meta-attention."

On this day, I was keenly aware of the different quality of attention that going without an agenda prompted in me. I am very good at listening. But we're all human, and it is natural for our attention to be divided at times. When I have a timed agenda, I listen to what other people are saying, yet at some level, I'm also thinking things like, *How are we doing on time? How do I segue to the next item on the agenda?*

Without an agenda, there was no split attention. I was free to throw myself wholly into the process of listening to and reading others and the room. It wasn't just the candor of their responses that generated material for the session; it was the quality of my own attention.

It is natural for the human brain to want to conserve energy. When we are in a routine or a process that feels comfortable and familiar, we settle into autopilot. We coast. That's not always bad. But shaking up your process and stripping away your safety nets (like an agenda) will almost always yield surprising and productive results. Like any experiment, it will generate fresh data, and that data will teach you something.

48

WITH PRIVILEGE COMES CHOICE

I am an optimistic person, yet I will also strike some cautionary notes. As I think I've made abundantly clear, the work of inclusive leadership is a long-haul effort. You will meet resistance—individual resistance and embedded institutional resistance. Sometimes, even with the best of intentions, inclusive initiatives lose their way.

Moreover, there is no getting around the fact that inclusive leadership means something different to those with more privilege and those with less, to those facing headwinds and those riding tailwinds. On the one hand, I believe in aspiring to an allyship in which we all feel a shared stake in the work—where we use the pronouns *we* and *us* and really mean it. However, while we can bridge difference, we can't erase it. Degree of privilege matters.

What do you do with the knowledge of your own degree of privilege? It can be tempting to feel guilty about the unearned privileges you've been afforded or to defend or deny those same privileges—or have a combination of all of this. I frequently see clients respond to conversations about privilege with anger, sadness, or confusion. These are natural, human responses. But just as in the work of recovering from mistakes we can get bogged down in the apology phase;* we can also get bogged down in the challenge of accepting our privilege. Accept it we must and then move on to the productive work of viewing that privilege as leverage to be used in the work of inclusion. If all that sounds too heady, keep it simple. Ask yourself: What is my privilege? What are my values? Are the choices I make (especially with how to leverage my privilege) aligned with my values?

With privilege comes the choice to engage in the work of inclusion (and all the messy issues it entails) or not to—at times, there may not appear to be a choice, but there very much is. Let me illustrate with a small but representative example.

After a JEDI© training, I received an anonymous note (which I encourage when it allows people to express their views more frankly) from an employee who said they didn't feel comfortable or safe in the sessions. They said, "I feel obligated to attend these sessions. And also obligated to accept what you say, even if I don't agree with it."

I thanked them for writing and sharing their feelings. I first clarified that psychological safety isn't the same as accepting everything we hear or even necessarily feeling comfortable. Part of psychological safety is feeling free to express discomfort, to push back, to *not* accept what may appear to be the consensus. And, I added, the sessions are not obligatory.

The person responded with a somewhat softened tone. They appreciated my willingness to hear different viewpoints. Their discomfort wasn't so much about me as about the company. "Work used to be a place where

---

* Which is not where the real work gets done; the priority is to repair and grow.

I could focus on . . . work. Not a place where I had to think about all of these contentious issues around race and other issues that are in the news. Now I have to think about it. Can't we just be adults and treat one another decently and get on with it?"

I shared this exchange with colleagues (with the employee's permission). My first impulse was to assume this was a white person. A friend challenged me: "Maybe it's a person of color and they're just overwhelmed by having to deal with this stuff 24/7 the rest of their life."

The employee and I continued to exchange notes, and she eventually shared her name. It did turn out to be a white woman. But I had learned a lesson not to jump to conclusions. Opting out isn't always what it appears to be.

I have seen this dynamic play out in a larger way at my own company, the RoundTable Institute. When I set out to build a team, my top priority was diversity in all its manifestations: social identity, geography, education, thought, and language, for example. After interviews, auditions, and reference checks, I initially invited a diverse group of thirty-six individuals to join RoundTable, assuming that there would be some turnover and we'd eventually settle on a team of around thirty committed facilitators. What I didn't anticipate was who would leave and why.

In the coaching industry, it's normal for people to subcontract with multiple boutique firms like RoundTable. It makes sense that people would pursue the firms that give them what they perceive to be the best opportunities. Like any industry, there's healthy and normal competition for the best talent, however you might define that. My priorities were to have a diverse team of absolutely outstanding coaches and facilitators, and to pay them very, very well—way above market rate. I also wanted my coaches and facilitators to choose the type of work they enjoyed, how often they worked, and if they wanted to work with any other firm.

After four months, the first person left. "I have found an opportunity that really sings to me, and it feels like a dream come true. I am so torn because I love the work you are building and what RoundTable stands for. I'm sorry." I was very happy for him even as I felt our loss.

A month later, another person shared a similar story with me. "I am so conflicted. I just love this work, but I have found a better opportunity."

A week after that, someone else left. "You are doing such important work, but I have to follow my heart and I've found a chance to do that."

To make a long story short, six months in, we had lost six facilitators and were left with what I believed was an incredible, smart, and diverse team . . . but with some glaring absences. When my office manager and I looked at the data, I was initially surprised to see that the people who left the team all had a few things in common: they all identified as white, heterosexual, college-educated, male, and American. We lost all our straight, white men. I looked at the data again and again to absorb and, frankly, accept this.

The people who remained on the team represented a range of identities: gay, Muslim, nonbinary, Black, woman of color, immigrant, disabled, global nomad, neurodiverse, only child, dual citizen, trans, high school dropout, and on and on. How can we make sense of the choice to stay and *do the work* or to leave? I know it's more complicated than a set of social identities. Headwinds and tailwinds got us to this place. There's an intersection of what we love to do, what we are good at, and what we need to do. But how do we explain that the only people who left all shared those particular (privileged) social identities?

My first guess is they had the choice and they exercised it. The choice to pursue work that they found more interesting or fulfilling. The choice to ask for what they needed—to use their voice and expect to be heard. I also recognize that those who stayed on the team also exercised their choice to stay. Yet it feels like a different level of choice, an entirely different kind of choice. It's harder to leave, I think, when your identity is tied up in the work. When it feels like the work implicates you personally and obviously. When you have privilege, you don't have to stay. You don't have to do the work. Perhaps you can move more freely, back and forth, along the LEAD identity continuum when you have privilege. You can continue to benefit from other people doing the work. You must examine yourself and ask if you are okay with that.

But indeed, choice and privilege do intersect in complicated ways.

On a personal level, as a woman of color with many headwinds and tailwinds, I feel I am constantly walking a line between making deliberate choices and feeling like I have a responsibility instead of a choice. One area where I don't feel I have any choice is having to deal with the daily microaggressions I encounter at work, in my neighborhood, at my kids' school, or at the gym. Having to face the constant threat of discrimination because of who I am is not something I have chosen for myself or for my kids.

For many, the toll of discrimination is so exhausting that sometimes we wish we could escape, give up, or not have to deal—just for one day. Sometimes, we simply don't have the resources to fight, whether in our workplaces or in our own families. At times, we feel others are making a choice for us when, with the best of intentions, they assume that people from underrepresented groups will take on a disproportionately large burden of responsibility in inclusion efforts on behalf of the company.

Even when our choices feel slim or constrained, we can find belonging and agency if we look within ourselves and amplify the parts of us that we can't deny to the world. We don't have a choice around the social threats of discrimination, bias, racism, sexism, or homophobia, for example. But we do have a choice around how we respond. I think of Mindy Kaling, the American actress, screenwriter, comedian, and producer who is of Indian descent.

"The moment I created my company," she says, "and my career became about making content that showcased stories of the underestimated and underrepresented, my entire life changed in the best ways. We are able to find unique perspectives we love, that make us cry and laugh, and give them a platform that has reached millions. I created Kaling International in my bed where I do all my writing because my beloved friend told me I needed a company to oversee the projects I was writing and producing. But in the past few years, it has become more than just the name. Besides my two kids, it is the love of my life."*

Each of us has something in us like that, something that feels undeniable; at some point, it builds so intensely that we have no choice but to free it and nurture it. For me, that is RoundTable.

One way to manage the lack of choice in dealing with the constant threat of exclusion and not belonging is to face it head on. Find the allies, be the ally, come together, and accept the challenge to do and be better—whether you've got tailwinds or headwinds. You don't have to (and shouldn't) do it alone for all of the reasons I described earlier: it's exhausting and you set yourself up for failure. When I started this work

---

* Mindy Kaling, Instagram, March 30, 2022, https://www.instagram.com/p/Cbu73GqLneb/?hl=en.

in 2011, I didn't know it would change my life in the best ways either. Though I had the tailwinds to give me many, many choices in my career, I gave myself few alternatives once I set the vision for spreading effective and inclusive leadership. It began to feel like an imperative, an absolute must. It is the experience of the Decided identity in the LEAD framework. And in that way, the lack of choice brought me personal fulfillment and yielded systemic change for many of our clients.

Yet I still struggle with the question of choice, in a deeply personal way. As I work on this chapter, I am trying to get my head around the incomprehensible fact that gun violence has become the leading cause of death among children in the United States. The fact hangs over me like a cloud, distracting me from the topic of privilege and choice. But as these words—privilege, choice, privilege, choice—swim in my brain, I begin to see a connection.

At the dinner table, where we have our most intimate conversations, I have told my children, "You can go anywhere in the world for college. Anywhere. I will support you. You don't have to stay in the United States. The world is open to you." What's unspoken is the subtext: *Leave. Go somewhere safe, where you are supported (maybe even celebrated) by the system, and where you—as brown people—can thrive, be yourself, and make a real difference in the world. Go find peace.*

I have the privilege to open up opportunities for my children, the freedom to give them a different life—a life that they can choose, a life where they can be and go global. They can leave what I feel is becoming an increasingly unsafe environment. I recognize that this is a highly privileged position. They don't *have* to stay. I recognize that exercising this option would be aligned with my values of safety and being a global citizen. I also hope that opening up this option for them pushes them to serve and spread justice. Will they share that privilege with others? Will they lend their hands to those who don't have the same privileges? Will they even see that? I certainly hope so. Of course that's my agenda, not theirs. But I have that privilege as a mom to influence and encourage along those lines, and dammit, I am using it to the max.

And yet . . . I stay here in the United States, as an immigrant, woman of color, and single mom, with a lot of work left to do. Why don't I go back to Canada? Why don't I leave? Why did I choose to live in Texas if I'm so concerned about gun violence? Why am I not exercising that privilege I talk about so fiercely with my kids? These are questions that keep me up at times, that I discuss regularly with my family and with my friends.

I don't have clear answers, but I do keep coming back to this idea: while in some ways I have many choices, in others I don't feel like I have a choice at all. For me, spreading the message of inclusive leadership is not just a calling, nor is it just a choice. It is very much a decision and a responsibility, a responsibility so deep and strong that at times I feel as though I don't have any other choice. It wouldn't be right of me to ignore this work; it wouldn't be aligned with my values or how I see the world. It is work that helps me reckon with my history, and it is work that I believe dismantles the oppression of my fellow human beings. So, I don't give myself another choice, even as I can see that I could have.

49

INCLUSIVE LEADERSHIP CAN'T BE ASSUMED

Yes, for me—and for a number of people, especially women of color—the work of inclusion feels like an imperative, the need so great, the stakes so personal. And yet we can never lose sight of the fact that, ultimately, it *is* a choice, and we must respect the right of people not to take on that role. Moreover, we must not assume that belonging to a historically excluded group necessarily translates into inclusive leadership. It may; but it also may not.

Making the wrong assumptions about someone's role in the fight for inclusion can set us up for disappointment. Worse, it can throw an entire organization's DEI work off track. It involves imposing our own narrative on someone else's self-determination—which of course runs completely counter to the spirit of inclusion.

I've witnessed the reins of an organization handed over to a woman of color who—whether by philosophy or temperament, it's not for me to say—did not make DEI a personal priority. Which is entirely her prerogative. Different leaders bring different strengths to the table.

We talked earlier about the difference between technical and adaptive challenges and how the work of inclusion tends to be more the latter.

Well, guess what? Some leaders are more gifted on the technical side of the equation. If that leader happens to be an underrepresented minority, those technical gifts may very well dictate their potential (and limitations) as a leader. It's okay for any underrepresented person not to take on inclusive leadership as a priority. That is their prerogative. Excluded and marginalized social identities come with enough baggage as it is. We should not add the assumption that they will take on certain causes to that baggage.

Yet we do make that assumption, all of the time. A CEO who is white and male is afforded a more extended learning curve, and also afforded more room to make mistakes. But a Black woman stepping into the same position brings an entirely different set of expectations, often unfairly. Even if DEI has not to date been a core part of her professional identity (or a core skill set—and it is a skill set, not just a belief or feeling), it is assumed that she will step up. The stakes are immediately higher, and the bar higher. She will be punished if she falters or doesn't step up. In a sense, she can't win either way. Here we need to be able to extend a different kind of grace, the grace of freedom not to symbolize a cause or issue unless we expressly choose to.

50

THE POWER OF ONE

've never met Dr. Tadataka Yamada, the focus of a wonderful article in the *Harvard Business Review* entitled "How One Person Can Change the Conscience of an Organization," but my guess is when he first began acting as an inclusive leader, he didn't think of himself as a leader. He was just doing the right thing. In this case, that meant advocating to diversify the gastroenterology faculty at the University of Michigan. Yamada specifically focused on helping more Black employees and women join the department. The authors of the article describe "challenging the status quo for the greater good" as a skill, a muscle.[*] Like any muscle, the more you use it, the stronger it gets.

By 2000, when Yamada was named the new chairman of research at the pharmaceutical giant GlaxoSmithKline (GSK), that muscle was well-exercised and ready for a greater challenge. Soon after starting at GSK, he found out that his new employer was one of thirty-nine pharmaceutical companies suing Nelson Mandela and the government of South

---

[*] Nicholas Eyrich, Robert Quinn, and David Fessell, "How One Person Can Change the Conscience of an Organization," *Harvard Business Review*, December 27, 2019.

Africa. The company claimed that South Africa, in its efforts to make antiretroviral drugs affordable to its people, had violated price protections and intellectual property rights.*

Yamada was horrified and felt strongly that the company was on the wrong side of the lawsuit, and the wrong side of history. But he didn't have a lot of formal influence at the time. He was new to the company, and although he was in charge of the science, he was not part of top leadership. He started small and quietly, talking to the research staff he worked with every day and knew best. He found that others felt as he did, but they also felt powerless to change things. Yamada persisted and began meeting one-on-one with individual board members. His message was simple: The company couldn't make life-saving medicines and then deny them to the people who needed them most. It was morally wrong and bad for the long-term success of the company.

Yamada's persistence and moral clarity won the day. Just a few months later, GSK and the other companies dropped their lawsuit. They dramatically cut the prices of their antiretroviral drugs. Moreover, with Yamada heading up the effort, one of GSK's laboratories was converted into a profit-exempt lab focused solely on eradicating diseases in the developing world. The company went from being on the wrong side of history to a global leader in health equity. Yamada himself would later go on to become President of the Global Health Program at the Bill and Melinda Gates Foundation.

The authors of the article cite a couple of key factors that enabled Dr.

---

* Nearly a quarter of these people were living with HIV/AIDS.

Yamada to leverage the power of one. First, the power of sequential skill building. When Yamada began quietly advocating for more diversity at the University of Michigan, he embarked on his own self-directed leadership-training course. He was exercising his voice and strengthening the muscle of challenging the status quo. He was making connections, expanding the platform of his network, and then leveraging that platform for good.

Second, the power of sustained focus and determination. As I've made clear throughout this book, inclusion is a long-term fight. There will be ups and downs, moments of frustration and disappointment. You're going up against a long history of bias and exclusion. But it's also a fight in which the tortoise, doggedly focused on small gains, can come out ahead.

Look around you. Make note of what's wrong and needs fixing. Of who is being left out and needs to be welcomed in. Bring the issue up with colleagues. Discuss how you can at least begin laying the foundation for change. Before you know it, the ball will be rolling. It may take a while for change to actually happen. But you will be on your way to becoming an inclusive leader, and that in itself is meaningful change.

THE LEGACY OF ONE

After I read the inspiring story of Dr. Tadataka Yamada, a client of mine immediately came to mind. I realized that he, too, very much exemplified the dynamic of the power of one—but in a different way, which I wish to explore here.

Like teachers, coaches aren't really supposed to have favorite clients. But some clients truly are rare and singular, and Remi was one of those. Remi was named chief diversity officer of a large research institute. It was a newly formed position at the organization, so the stakes were high, and Remi understood that. He had been recruited specifically for this role because of his previous experience in building diversity and inclusion initiatives at similar institutions.

In his first year, Remi socialized a new language of inclusion at the institute. It is one thing to create such a language; it is another thing for people to actually use it and for it to become normalized. Remi had a special touch for making that happen. Part of his secret was his skill in building a team to rally behind his vision. They were stalwart in their loyalty to Remi. It was more than just his compelling vision. It was his delivery and presence that helped people feel seen, understood, and appreciated in a way only Remi could offer. He was warm, kind, generous, direct, and hilarious. Those qualities are a gift, and Remi had it in spades.

We talk a lot at RoundTable about the power of one person to create truly significant change. We want our clients to understand they have influence over others—whether or not they think of themselves as leaders, whether or not they like it, whether or not they want to own that influence. Influence is leverage, which is power. And they have a choice (actually, a series of choices) about how to use that leverage.

Many of our clients take that message seriously. But they also understand, and we do as well, that without institutional support—in the form of title, resources, and systems—sustainable culture change is not always possible. Remi had all of that support and understood the opportunity before him. In the short eight months I had the chance to work with him, I saw the power of one (which we talk a lot about in theory, but which is rarely fully realized in practice) play out dramatically before my very eyes. In that short time, he led provocative lunch discussions that encouraged people to share their personal stories of discrimination. He facilitated town-hall discussions and a listening tour days after Daunte Wright's murder in Minneapolis in 2021. He invited authors and speakers to come to the institute and talk about diversity and inclusion. He drafted op-eds, mission statements, and media releases covering the institute's commitments and actions toward building an inclusive workplace. He started necessary conversations and continued them. Most people at the institute agreed that the culture was changing, largely because of Remi's actions and commitment.

There is a flipside to the power of one. When that person is so rarely gifted, and when that gift is paired with real power and influence, what happens when they are no longer around? People leave, people retire, life happens. Will the changes be sustained, the inspiration lasting? What happens when one person disproportionately carries the torch for inclusion?

Inexplicably and tragically, one year into Remi's tenure, we were forced to ask ourselves that very question. On a Monday morning, I opened up my inbox to read a note from his manager explaining that over the weekend, Remi had suddenly and unexpectedly passed away. My mind raced. I thought of all of the people whose lives he had touched, who followed and depended on him and his vision. I knew that for many, many people, Remi was the reason they counted.

In the wake of a sudden loss like this, uncertainty arises. And with uncertainty, fear raises its ugly head. Fear whispers in our ear, raising doubts, making us wonder if we belong or if we're good enough. Remi's team started asking questions: Am I still allowed to run my brown-bag lunch for the Latinx ERG? Can we still proceed with our plans for Black History Month, or will they take our funding away? The team felt they had one and only one champion: Remi. Now he was gone. They worried that their efforts would lose direction, that they wouldn't matter.

If this kind of loss is the flipside to the power of one, compassion is the flipside to fear. Where there is fear, there is compassion. I watched as the senior leadership team rallied around Remi's vision and team, and reassured them that all of their initiatives were valued and would continue to be valued. If anything, they upped the ante on their commitment, pouring even more effort and attention into the institute's DEI initiatives. Whether they thought about it this way or not, it seemed as if the leadership team was absorbing Remi's role and legacy and spreading it among themselves. They were imitating him, emulating him, sharing what he had left.

What had he left? A certain intangible "just enough" to carry the mission forward and build on it. I think that's what great leaders do. They leave you inspired, with just enough tools to create and follow through on a vision so that you can make it your own.

51

THE POWER OF TWO

In both my examples of the power of one, that individual had advantages that a chief executive does not. When an employee from the rank-and-file speaks up, their individual moral authority can carry great weight. Their initiative has nothing to do with their title or job description. This is truly the power of one in evidence in its purest form.

Yet a leader whose designated role is to advance diversity, equity, and inclusion has advantages as well. They do not have to balance potentially competing objectives in other facets of the business. Their sole charge is to create a more inclusive workplace. The rest of the organization turns to them to model the best inclusive practices. That is their area of expertise. And those are the grounds on which their success will be measured. Accountability, when it is fully embraced, can be a real source of leverage and power.

However, that accountability—when it is not shared by others, especially the chief executive—can be a double-edged sword. A recent survey found that, on issues of race and racism, the *least* trusted person in many organizations was . . . the company's chief diversity officer. It is not that these officers lack commitment; they are not being set up to succeed. Moreover, while such roles are seeing a great deal of growth, they are also seeing enormous turnover. This tells me that, in too many cases, the person charged with overseeing DEI is being left alone on an island. They are being given accountability without meaningful strategic power. As Human Resources departments are so much of the time, DEI is left siloed and isolated.

This unfortunate dynamic illustrates a lack of what we might call the Power of Two: a necessary collaboration and synergy between the chief executive and the person designated with overseeing DEI. Let me briefly share two contrasting stories to illustrate. In the first instance, while the CEO embraced the work of inclusive leadership without reservation (he has appeared in several of my stories), he was also smart and humble enough to know that it was best if someone else in the company was the visible face of DEI. He also realized this was an opportunity to address several organizational issues with one bold move.

The best candidate for the position was Aisha, his vice president of Human Resources. For a host of reasons (the perception of HR as a "feminine" position among them), the head of HR is rarely a C-level executive position. And candidates for CEO almost never come from an HR background. In this case, despite a real commitment to inclusion, the CEO knew that his senior leadership team was decidedly not diverse. By putting Aisha in charge of DEI and of shepherding the JEDI© program at the company, he diversified his leadership team and elevated the Human Resources department.

The arrangement worked, and it became more than just a symbolic appointment, for several reasons. First, the CEO and Aisha had already established a bond of trust and psychological safety. She jumped into the new role with both feet and wasn't afraid to stand her ground when the CEO challenged her; and he, for his part, deferred to her leadership. He also invested in her by hiring me to work one-on-one with both of them for six months. In a variety of ways, he signaled her value to him and the company; he signaled that he had her back and would not leave her hanging.

In the second story (a very personal story with which I end this section of the book), Jay, an inspired chief diversity officer arrived at his new employer . . . only to find that the person who had hired him and who he expected to report to had quit. So he began his tenure on unsteady ground, feeling the rug had been pulled out from under him. He quickly established a good rapport with the chief operating officer, who he would now report to. But the COO went beyond simply empowering him. She said to him, in essence, "You will be the face of DEI at this organization; you will take the lead. But I want and need to go on my own inclusive journey as well. If I'm going to hold you accountable, I need to know these issues in a much deeper way, and I realize it's not your job to educate me."

She took it upon herself to get up to speed. She read, she joined an anti-racism group, she asked questions, she listened. Her initiative transformed their relationship from one of mere delegation to one of active collaboration and partnership. Both can work. But when the person holding organizational power is willing to get their hands dirty and shows they have skin in the game, the dynamic changes.* Among other things, it also signals to the rest of the organization that DEI is a top strategic priority.

It also helped that Jay had an additional, unexpected ally: someone with influence in the organization and to whom he was linked by random circumstance—a shared hair stylist. I mention that linkage not to slight it but to underscore the serendipity of human connection and leverage: we never know what common ground might allow us to lift our voice on

---

* Usually the person in power is the CEO; this was a special case.

behalf of another (or vice versa). Change can depend on links that appear random until we imbue them with meaning.

While change coming from the top is often a good thing, even better is when change is pushed by top leadership *and* by people throughout the organizations—the Power of Many.

The Power of One is bolstered by the Power of Two, which might depend in subtle ways on the Power of Three. In the end, the Power of One is always buoyed by the Power of Many. It takes all of us.

CONCLUSION

In this book, I've tried to keep things simple and relatable and to root the principles I present in example and story. But there's no getting around it: making our workplaces and our world more inclusive is a huge challenge. You may still feel somewhat daunted by it all. Or simply not be clear about what to do next.

When in doubt, return to chapter 30 and ask yourself where you are on the LEAD continuum—again, keep in mind that this is typically not a linear, one-time path but more of a repeating cycle. Do you identify with the questions and tensions in Launch? Experiment? Activate? Decide?

Once you've done that, pick one skill, one leadership muscle to focus on. For example, it never hurts to work on your listening skills. Listening leads to changed conversations. And changed conversations lead to opened minds, to new behavior, and to different results.

RAPPORT

This segues nicely into the first of three capacities that have, over the years, kept me grounded and on course: creating *rapport*. This is central to my work as a coach, as well as critical for all leadership and for cultivating an inclusive organizational culture. Throughout this book, I have discussed the importance of relationships. I have found that great relationships—through trust, safety, shared history, and, frankly, love—give me latitude and grace to experiment and take risks.

As you well know by now, experimentation and risk-taking are integral in my approach to inclusive leadership. Great relationships offer a safety net for what can sometimes feel like a high-wire act. You can step up and speak up knowing that you're going to make mistakes but you have a soft place to land. You will be able to fall back on the trust and mutual respect you have cultivated with others. You will be able to talk it out, repair as needed, move on with the work, make things better, and *be* better. In the context of great relationships, mistakes that might otherwise seem difficult to bounce back from become small, recoverable errors; they become learning opportunities to embrace.

All the aspects of the LEAD framework lean heavily on relationships, and relationships start with building rapport. It's a skill that can be learned (though some people have it naturally), and I'm going to summarize it very simply: rapport is built through your energy. It's about coming to someone with genuine positivity and interest, projecting a spirit of welcome and invitation. These intentions can mean a world of difference and likely matter more to someone else than you could ever know. The first time you meet someone, use their name. Get the pronunciation and tone right. A genuine smile matters. A lot. These are the building blocks of connection.

One of the best ways to practice connecting with people is, counterintuitively, with strangers. When you check out at the grocery store, smile and thank the clerk. Maybe ask them how they are doing—with genuine interest in their response. Sometimes we hesitate to do this because we think the other person is scowling, busy, or uninterested in us. Instead of assuming a moment of connection will be unwelcome, assume the opposite. Shift your approach, bring in a new energy, and see what happens. These kinds of small experiments may not be easy for you. But over time, you will get better at it, and you will notice the ripple effects that come from these overtures. Building rapport with people—strangers, friends, family, colleagues—is cumulative. It may not feel like much in the moment. But in every act of invitation, you sow a seed of inclusion.

This kind of overture, while it can be significant, is just a first step. As a way of illustrating how to deepen rapport, let me share my process of creating connection with prospective clients. Well before a JEDI© workshop begins, I will typically spend quite a bit of time with the leader of a company. I, of course, want to hear about the company and its culture, where the leadership is on their journey of inclusive leadership, and what they are looking to get out of JEDI.© But most of all, it's about a one-on-one connection. I usually start off by sharing something about myself and where I'm at. This kind of voluntary self-disclosure models vulnerability and also gives the other person implicit permission to share and be vulnerable.*

Maybe the most important thing I do, aside from modeling vulnerability, is communicate the lack of a specific agenda. I'll say something like, "Let's see where the next hour takes us . . ." There is tremendous power in

---

* There is a whole body of research around what is called the "psychology of self-disclosure." It's a reciprocal process in which, by gradually sharing experiences and emotions, and listening to the other do the same, we build understanding and trust.

such a simple, open-ended statement like this, in presenting a significant block of time as a truly blank canvas. This doesn't mean I'm not prepared or haven't done my research, though. I'm clear and focused, but also agile. So often, business meetings are about agendas and talking points. Such guardrails can be useful at times, but they also lead to people staying close to predetermined scripts and playbooks. That's not the place where risk and real connection live, and it's not where my best work happens. As I found out when my co-facilitator and I threw out an entire day's agenda and let listening create the agenda, removing the safety net often brings out the best in people.

A related thing I do is to make it clear that it's okay to not be so entirely "buttoned up." People in business are used to feeling they have to project a certain professional persona, especially with someone they are meeting for the first time. When I meet with a CEO, they quickly get the sense from me that it's all right to drop that persona, to let their guard down. I know the business world and can speak the language. I have built a very successful business myself. But I am still that woman my fellow coaching trainee and future boss mistook for a yoga instructor. The absence of a strict agenda and the permission to reveal one's real and sometimes messy self is something some clients find tremendously liberating and disarming. Others will, at first, be taken aback a bit. I don't wish to make anyone uncomfortable, but I do want them to find it a little risky. (After all, if they are going to fully commit to inclusive leadership, the risks have only just begun.) To me, this is about our shared humanity. Maybe that morning I stepped in a puddle, your coffee went cold, she got a new Chapstick that she's excited about, or they forgot their wallet. These are the pieces of connection that I like to bring to the surface so that we can share in the realness of our personal experiences. Such conversations are disarming; they level the playing field and subdue unhelpful power dynamics. When I share a tiny bit about my day, you will too. And then we start to build trust and connection.

What's fascinating is that, regardless of their personality or initial reaction to the tone I set, these CEOs almost invariably take the reins and run with the invitation I have implicitly extended to them. I will get the ball rolling by sharing, but they will often speak for a good thirty-five or forty minutes of the hour. They will surprise themselves. The core message I send—*I get you, I'm with you*—sets them free.

It may seem like an odd comparison, but recently I was watching Jane Goodall speak about her unorthodox approach to building rapport with the chimpanzees she famously studied. Rather than (as was the traditional playbook) adopt the role of distant observer, Jane thought of herself as a neighbor. Instead of trying to dissect the chimpanzees' behavior, her guiding impulse was simply to honor their experience. She said, "I see you, I hear you." She let them be themselves. This is ultimately what rapport is all about.

EQUANIMITY

Staying focused on relationships—on building them, on deepening them—also helps me develop the *equanimity* that makes my work both sustainable and enjoyable. If rapport is the entry point to connection, then equanimity is the enduring force. But why *equanimity* and not a simpler term like *neutrality, composure,* or *poise*? Because there is a special nuance to equanimity. I accept you *and* I accept me—our strengths, our weaknesses, our mistakes. I maintain connection to you without the pressure to change who I am so that you can feel better about who you are. I preserve myself, my opinions, my beliefs, and my perspectives while inviting you to do the same. It is at once interpersonal and intrapersonal. None of those other words offer that elegant nuance.

So how do you "do" equanimity? Equanimity starts with curiosity, compassion, and awareness. When we are truly curious, we suspend judgment and assumption. Compassion—the understanding that we all struggle and suffer and are deserving of love—allows you to express care and concern for others while remaining separate and not fully consumed by their experience. Awareness helps you to see both the suffering and wholeness in yourself and others. Without that awareness, you can't be compassionate or curious. From a place of equanimity, you can express care and concern while acknowledging difference—difference of opinion, difference of experience. As with rapport, an accepting presence is critical. Equanimity is about finding balance between compassion and impartiality.

For me, equanimity is not just an ideal or aspiration but a mindset and a concrete practice. It starts with the physical: both the physicality that I inhabit for myself and the body language I present to others. Our bodies tell others what our mindset is; they also nudge us toward a certain mindset. The physical posture of equanimity is grounded and firm. In my eye contact, tone of voice, and other physical cues, I project invitation and a degree of vulnerability. But also calm. Calm is distinct from neutral, in that I am not distant. I am very much engaged and very much have an agenda, which is to connect and explore. But the energy I bring to that connection is calm, not charged. I am calm because of my focus, which is on connection, on learning, on teaching.

Early on in my coaching career, and early on in the development of RoundTable, I went through difficult sessions that really tested me and that also forged my resolve to cultivate this necessary quality of equanimity. I lost my equanimity when I lost my calm and when I lost my focus. When I maintain my focus on reciprocal connection, I am able to stand in the fire. I stand in the fire, and the heat of whatever resistance I am meeting doesn't touch me. I am focused on creating clarity in the heat of the moment. Resistance and friction offer useful energy, but they also muddle the air and create a mess. My job is to clear the air and create clarity. I have to be implacable to stay calm and stand in the fire.

And I have to believe. I have to see beyond the mess and believe that together, with grace, we can walk through the fire and get to clearer air—that we can find the clarity where connection and change happen. I have to believe in my own agency in this process, that I can hold space for opposition, for resistance, for harmony, for agreement and disagreement, for alignment and misalignment, for the mess, and for the clearing.

Mindset is powerful, but it is also delicate. I know that if I falter in any of these—my physicality, my focus, my belief—my equanimity will waver. I know I have to cultivate and reaffirm that equanimity mindset on a daily basis. Like setting an intention before yoga or meditation, it is for me a daily practice.

COURAGE

Rapport and equanimity depend on the third pillar: *courage*. Without courage, we cannot take the first step. Connecting with others, committing to change, admitting you messed up, repairing fractures, and reworking your beliefs—it is all hard, and it is all profound. It all starts with courage. Courage, in turn, is bolstered by rapport and equanimity. Relationships and connection sustain me. An equanimous mindset keeps me grounded and moving forward.

What also helps is knowing that inclusive leadership is a path not a destination. As cliché as it may be, the "path" metaphor eases me into my fallibility, allowing me to explore rather than be perfect. In my mind, I see the path as meandering and twisting, smooth at times and bumpy at others. I see colorful flowers and vegetation. I see hidden off-shoot path-ways, some inviting and others foreboding. The path feels at times familiar and at times completely unknown. It's hard for me, a goal-oriented person and recovering overachiever, to adopt a "path" versus "destination" lens. But it has given me an immense amount of grace and forgiveness—for myself and others. Courage means you acknowledge your fear, confront it, and accept the consequences of your errors. It means taking the risk with no guarantee of the outcome. It means accepting that you might experience great joy and love just as much as you might mess up, cause harm, or feel deep pain. The work of inclusion depends on your courage.

Courage starts small. To bring this book full circle, I have stated early and often the following principle: Great leaders know their own stories. Really well. And courageously share them. *Courageously* was a late addi-tion. Telling your story may not, at first, sound like a courageous act, but it is. It was hard for me to feature my own story as much as I did. In the business and professional world, we have all adopted the language of vulnerability—but how often do we truly practice it? Truly let our guard down? Truly disarm ourselves of our defenses?

I told you about my dear client Remi. Every time he introduced himself to someone new, he would say, "My name is Remi Amani. My pronouns are he/him. I'm a first-generation immigrant and the first in my family to go to college. I'm an MD and PhD, and I went to UCLA." It is an unusual way to introduce oneself. But it gave others permission to reciprocate. Soon after Remi was named chief diversity officer of the orga-nization where I met him and would run a series of JEDI© workshops, it became normal for people to share their pronouns and something telling and revealing about themselves. People who had worked together for years suddenly related to one another in a less guarded way. With one small (and yes, courageous) act, Remi had expanded the psychological safety of the organization and changed the culture.

———

The work of inclusive leadership is deeply personal for me. If that means I feel the ups and downs of the work more keenly, so be it. I also know this: when the motivation is personal, the effort is more fulfilling and more sustainable. That's why I started this book with my own story. You have your own stories. They can make the work personal for you; they can fuel and sustain your journey. I encourage you to dig into those memories, to get comfortable with them, to make them a part of your identity. Sometimes as professionals we focus only on our adult stories, and neglect the early, foundational ones: our origin stories. When you were a child learning about the world, you hopefully experienced acceptance, love, and warmth. But you also surely experienced pain and exclusion—your first understanding of what injustice means. You learned in a visceral way just how powerful it is for someone to say: I get you, I'm with you.

Take your stories and your own personal mission of inclusion out into the world. With them, you can create change and thrive.

REFERENCES

Annie E. Casey Foundation. *Race Equity and Inclusion Action Guide: 7 Steps to Advance and Embed Race Equity and Inclusion Within Your Organization.* 2014. https://assets.aecf.org/m/resourcedoc/ AECF_EmbracingEquity7Steps-2014.pdf.

Bohnet, Iris. *What Works: Gender Equality by Design.* Cambridge: Harvard University Press, 2016.

Bridges, William. *Managing Transitions: Making the Most of Change.* Reading, MA: Addison-Wesley, 1991.

Brown, Jennifer. "From Unaware to Accomplice: The Ally Continuum." Minisode #14, *The Will to Change*, podcast. June 2018.

Chugh, Dolly. *The Person You Mean to Be: How Good People Fight Bias.* New York: Harper Business, 2018.

Cooper, Marianne. "Women Leaders Took on Even More Invisible Work During the Pandemic." *Harvard Business Review*, October 13, 2021.

David, Cliff, and Barbara Steel. "How Focusing on Feedback Can Unlock Better Performance." NeuroLeadership Institute, November 5, 2020.

Edmondson, Amy. "Psychological Safety and Learning Behavior in Work

Teams." *Administrative Science Quarterly* 44, no. 2 (1999): 350–383. https://doi.org/10.2307/2666999.

Ely, Robin, and David A. Thomas. "Getting Serious about Diversity: Enough Already with the Business Case." *Harvard Business Review* 98, no. 6 (November-December 2020): 114–122.

Emre, Merve. "The Repressive Politics of Emotional Intelligence." *New Yorker*, April 19, 2021.

Eyrich, Nicholas, Robert Quinn, and David Fessell. "How One Person Can Change the Conscience of an Organization." *Harvard Business Review*, December 27, 2019.

Forscher, Patrick, Calvin Lai, Jordan Axt, Charles Ebersole, Michelle Herman, Patricia Devine, and Brian Nosek. "A Meta-analysis of Procedures to Change Implicit Measures." *Journal of Personality and Social Psychology* 117, no. 3 (September 2019): 522–559.

Forscher, Patrick, Chelsea Mitamura, Emily Dix, William Cox, Patricia Devine. "Breaking the Prejudice Habit: Mechanisms, Timecourse, and Longevity." *Journal of Experimental Social Psychology*, no. 72 (2017): 133–146.

Ho, Melanie. *Beyond Leaning In: Gender Equity and What Organizations are Up Against*. Strategic Imagination, 2021.

Hochschild, Arlie Russell. *The Managed Heart*. Berkeley: University of California Press, 1983.

Hsu, Hua. "The Soft Racism of Apu from *The Simpsons*." *New Yorker*, November 16, 2017. https://www.newyorker.com/culture/cultural-comment/the-soft-racism-of-apu-from-the-simpsons.

Kahneman, Daniel. *Thinking, Fast and Slow*. Farrar, Straus and Giroux, 2011.

Kaling, Mindy. "In Season 7 of *The Office*." Instagram, March 30, 2022. https://www.instagram.com/p/Cbu73GqLneb/?hl=en.

Kondabolu, Hari. *The Problem with Apu.* Directed by Michael Melamedoff. truTV, 2017.

LeanIn.org and McKinsey & Company. *Women in the Workplace 2022 Report.* https://www.mckinsey.com/featured-insights/diversity-and-inclusion/women-in-the-workplace.

Lee, Edmond, and Ben Smith. "Axios Allows Its Reporters to Join Protests." *New York Times*, June 8, 2020. https://www.nytimes.com/2020/06/08/business/media/axios-allows-reporters-protest-march.html.

Lerner, Harriet. *Why Won't You Apologize? Healing Big Betrayals and Everyday Hurts.* UK: Gallery Books, 2017.

Lucas, George, dir. *Star Wars: Episode IV - A New Hope.* Produced by Gary Kurtz. 1977; Twentieth Century Fox, Lucasfilm.

McMurtrie, Beth. "Teaching: Is It Time to Redefine Class Participation?" Newsletter, *Chronicle of Higher Education*, September 8, 2022.

Meade, Michael. "The March of Violence." Episode 135, *Mosaic Voices*, podcast.

Mesquita, Batja. *Between Us: How Cultures Create Emotions.* UK: WW Norton, 2022.

Moynihan, Daniel Patrick. *The Negro Family: The Case for National Action.* Office of Policy Planning and Research, United States Department of Labor. March 1965.

New York Times Magazine (online). "The 1619 Project." Accessed June 24, 2023. https://www.nytimes.com/interactive/2019/08/14/magazine/11619-america-slavery.html.

Noah, Trevor. "Lizzo's 'Grrrls' Lyric Controversy: Between the Scenes." *The Daily Show*, July 28, 2022. https://www.youtube.com/watch?v=ejBRBZWnotQ.

Pettersen, William. "Success Story, Japanese American Style." *New York*

Times Magazine, January 9, 1966.

Powers, Lauren. *How to Listen Out Loud: Ridiculously Powerful Skills for Leading, Relating, and Happifying.* Pluck Publications, 2023.

Purushothaman, Deepa. *The First, the Few, the Only: How Women of Color Can Redefine Power in Corporate America.* HarperCollins, 2022.

Rhimes, Shonda. "Shonda Rhimes Teaches Writing for Television." MasterClass series. Accessed June 25, 2023. https://www.masterclass.com/classes/shonda-rhimes-teaches-writing-for-television.

Rock, David, Beth Jones, and Chris Weller. "Using Neuroscience to Make Feedback Work and Feel Better." *Strategy and Business*, no. 93 (August 27, 2018). https://www.strategy-business.com/article/Using-Neuroscience-to-Make-Feedback-Work-and-Feel-Better.

Sedaris, David. "David Sedaris on Coming Out, All Over Again." CBS News, October, 16, 2022. https://www.cbsnews.com/video/david-sedaris-on-coming-out-all-over-again/.

Taleb, Nassim Nicholas. *Antifragile: Things That Gain from Disorder.* New York: Random House Publishing Group, 2014.

Thaler, Richard H., and Cass R. Sunstein. *Nudge.* New York: Penguin, 2009.

Wagner, Laura. "Axios to Staff: Our Values Are Cynically Engineered and Incoherent." *Defector*, May 11, 2022. https://defector.com/axios-to-staff-our-values-are-cynically-engineered-and-incoherent.

Wong, Alice, ed. *Disability Visibility.* New York: Crown Books, 2020.

Yoon, Hannah. "How to Respond to Microaggressions." *New Yorker*, March 3, 2020. https://www.nytimes.com/2020/03/03/smarter-living/how-to-respond-to-microaggressions.html.

ACKNOWLEDGMENTS

Although it might seem that I wrote this book all by myself, I most certainly did not. First of all, Scott Doyle's words and ideas appear throughout these pages, our collaboration so close and effective that it's hard to know which words are whose. Lauren Magnussen and Dayna Jackson round out my team of writing minds and editors. If you're writing anything, please find yourself a brilliant writing team like this; they will make the process fun and smooth, and the final product will be much better than you could have expected.

Anjali and Zayn gave me words and ideas and inspiration for this book while on our drives to sports practices, tabla recitals, and drama club meetings, and in our travels to New York, London, Ottawa, and Paris (and many more to come!). Millu, thanks for reminding all of us what's important in life: playing with trucks, being loud, and hugging hard. Mom, Dad, and Sonal, thank you for remembering details of the early days and for knowing I could get here.

Beyond reminding me to stock up on good snacks and go for a swim, Lakshmi Balachandra has encouraged, challenged, understood, loved, pushed, scolded, heard, and held me every step of the way. Nothing compares to your friendship, Lakshmi. Every conversation and Thursday evening date with André Key over the past four years clarified and expanded my ideas in this book. "You don't even know" how much I have felt uplifted, accepted, and loved by you. My girlfriends Alejandra Adán, Erika Himes, and Suchi Garg let me know when to take life seriously and when not to; they are among the smartest women I've ever known. I have the best coach friends in the world: Ben Olds, Deb Grayson Riegel, Mark Zumwalt, and Signý Wilson keep me laughing, inquiring, puzzling, and dreaming in ways that bolster me and help me to feel so deeply cared for. My BIPOC coaches' group and Deep Democracy community have been very important sources of inspiration and connection and I'm thankful for our regular calls. And to the leaders in my Women's Presidents Organization group who championed and supported me from the moment you saw the book design, thank you.

For believing in me, this book, and in JEDI for Leaders,© I have many clients, colleagues, and mentors to thank including Martha Miser, Lauren Powers, Jonathan Cross, Annie Collins, Abbas Kazimi, Diane Melchionne, Yakiry Malena Adal, Carrie Gilman, Aremin Hacobian, Christina Miser, Nina Simonds, Chris Powell, Tiffani Santagati, Stacy Parson, Luis Rodriguez, Jeff Brimhall, Casey Harless, Ayman Kaheel, Angie O'Donnell, Suzanne Alonzo, Jenny Strauss, Johannes Gehrke, Wendy Taylor Wampler, Toshinori Hisamune, Walt Kowtoniuk, Abbie Celniker, Bob Selman, and Elaine Blais. Jeremy Cook: you were the one who planted the seed for this book at a Priya Session back in 2016. I finally heard you. Thank you! The fantastic facilitators at RoundTable and my heroic admin team past and present including Shannon Elder, Khrysmalein Licay, and Kelley Rose: you're all such wonderful human beings!

Finally, a shout-out to the glorious stumbles, foibles, and oh-no's I've had over the years: clearly, old friends, you were the inspiration for this book. To everyone who considered picking up this book and reading it, thank you. We're all on this journey together.

ABOUT THE AUTHOR

Dr. Priya Nalkur is the president of the RoundTable Institute, a research and coaching firm dedicated to developing inclusive leaders, communities, and workplaces. She is the creator of the JEDI Leadership Development Series,© a training program that has helped thousands of leaders around the world realize their leadership potential. A Harvard- and Yale-educated psychologist, she is an expert in dialogue, facilitation, motivation, and coaching. Priya finds inspiration in her fearless girlfriends, long hikes and mountain climbs, kitchen dance parties with her two children, and beautiful, adventurous writing.